CONTENTS

Introduction   2

Mastering Time Management   26

Cultivating Resilience   41

Fostering Innovative Thinking   54

Building Strong Relationships   66

Developing a Growth Mindset   81

Taking Calculated Risks   94

Creating a Wealth Mindset   107

Practicing Discipline and Consistency   122

Embracing Continuous Learning   138

Giving Back and Making a Difference   152

Conclusion   164

THE 10 HABITS OF BILLIONAIRES

EXPLORE BILLIONAIRE HABITS FOR PERSONAL AND FINANCIAL SUCCESS WITH ACTIONABLE INSIGHTS ON MINDSET, TIME MANAGEMENT, AND RESILIENCE

INTRODUCTION

The Power of Habit

Our lives are constructed by our habits. They influence our behavior, direct our course, and eventually shape who we are. The strength of habits lies in their capacity to improve our lives and bring about long-lasting change. In "The 10

Habits of Billionaires: Powerful Lessons in Personal Change," we examine the behaviors that have enabled billionaires to achieve incredible success and discuss how anyone looking to improve themselves financially and personally can adopt these behaviors.

1. The Loop of Habits

   We must first comprehend how habits are created in order to appreciate their potency. Three essential elements make up a habit loop: the trigger, the routine, and the reward. The routine is the activity itself; the reward is the reinforcement of the habit through positive reinforcement; and the cue initiates the habit. Knowing this loop will help us recognize and change our own patterns.

2. The Combined Impact

   The compounding influence of habits is one of their most potent features. Significant outcomes can be achieved over time by engaging in small, regular activities. Billionaires are aware of this idea and take advantage of it. They understand that building a daily routine that supports their objectives is what leads to success, rather than achieving it quickly. Through persistently engaging in constructive routines, they generate a domino effect that drives them toward achievement.

3. Crucial Behaviors

   Not every habit is made equally. Our lives are impacted by some habits more than others. We refer to these as "keystone habits." Adopting keystone habits can have a positive impact on various aspects of our lives. For instance, consistent exercise is a foundational habit that enhances mental clarity and discipline in addition to physical health. Through the identification and cultivation of keystone habits, we can generate a cascade effect that enhances multiple facets of our lives.

4. The Influence of Regularity
Billionaires know how crucial rituals are to preserving discipline and regularity. They create daily routines that support their values and objectives, which helps them stay concentrated and productive. Establishing routines gives tasks structure and reduces decision fatigue, which frees up mental energy for other critical activities. Positive habits can help us build a strong foundation for success by introducing them into our everyday routines.

5. Stacking Habits
Billionaires utilize a strategy called habit stacking to increase the productivity of their routines. It entails establishing a sequence of events that eventually become automatic by connecting a new habit to an already-existing one. If your objective is to read more books, for instance, you can combine the habit of reading with your current morning coffee-drinking behavior. When you combine the two activities on a regular basis, reading fits in naturally with your everyday schedule. By using our current habits to form new ones, habit stacking makes it simpler to adopt and sustain healthy lifestyle choices.

6. The Influence of Mentality
Although habits have a significant role in success, they are not the only factor. The way millionaires think contributes significantly to their success. They have a growth mentality, meaning they

think that with commitment and effort, they can improve their skills and intelligence. They are able to rise to challenges, persevere in the face of setbacks, and see failure as a teaching moment because of this perspective. We can transcend self-limiting beliefs and reach our full potential by developing a growth mindset.

7. The Significance of Introspection
A crucial element in the creation of habits is self-awareness. It entails being aware of our advantages, disadvantages, and the things that set off particular behaviors in us. We can choose to alter and get better at what we do by being conscious of our habits and the reasons that drive them. Self-awareness is a top priority for billionaires, who routinely evaluate their behavior and solicit input to pinpoint areas in which they may improve. We can break free from unfavorable patterns and form habits that support our objectives by becoming more self-aware.

8. The significance of accountability
Accountability is an effective technique for creating habits. Billionaires know how important it is to surround themselves with people who make them accountable for their deeds. Having a coach, mentor, or accountability partner makes it more likely that you will maintain your positive habits. By letting others know about our objectives and advancements, we inspire accountability and drive to finish what we start. Accountability offers the motivation and support required to stay on course and succeed in the long run.

9. The Way to Long-Term Transformation
Persistence and dedication are necessary for

forming new habits and bringing about long-lasting transformation. There will inevitably be setbacks, and it is not always easy. We may, however, overcome obstacles and bring about long-lasting change by realizing the power of habits and putting methods in place to encourage habit formation. The book "The 10 Habits of Billionaires: Powerful Lessons in Personal Change" offers the motivation, wisdom, and resources required to start a life-changing path toward both financial and personal success. We can live abundant and fulfilled lives and reach our full potential through the power of habits.

Billionaires' Mentalities

In the search for an understanding of billionaires' extraordinary success, it becomes clear that their accomplishments are not exclusively due to financial acumen or business expertise. Instead, a major component of their success is the elaborate tapestry of their mentalities—the deeply entrenched thought patterns that distinguish them from the rest. This part dives into the vast reservoir of billionaires' mentalities, revealing the profound insights that have catapulted them to the pinnacle of achievement.

Billionaires possess a unique ability to envision the future. They have a visionary attitude that looks beyond current issues, allowing them to identify opportunities where others see obstacles. By maintaining a forward-thinking mindset, they transcend the restrictions of the present, continuously pushing the limits of what is possible.

Billionaires are known for their high-risk tolerance and mastery of fear. Rather than submitting to fear, they overcome it. Dread of failure, dread of the unknown these are obstacles that billionaires not only overcome but also use to their advantage. This mental fortitude enables them to make ambitious decisions, which frequently result in revolutionary achievement.

Billionaires exhibit unwavering self-belief, bordering on boldness. They have steadfast confidence in themselves and their talents, allowing them to face obstacles with composure and determination. This unwavering self-confidence serves as a catalyst for success, pulling people onward even in the face of seemingly insurmountable challenges.

Successful billionaires excel at adapting to change and learning continuously. They recognize that in a continually changing world, stagnation is synonymous with regression. They keep ahead of the curve by adopting a culture of constant learning and acquiring new skills and insights to bolster their mental arsenal against the ever-changing tides of industry and innovation.

Resilience in the Face of Setbacks: Billionaires view setbacks and failures as opportunities rather than obstacles. Their mental resilience allows them to see setbacks as chances for growth and refinement. Instead of obsessing over failures, they learn vital lessons and use their newfound understanding and determination to prepare for the next initiative.

Billionaires know the value of smart networking and relationship-building. Their mindsets are geared toward forming meaningful partnerships that extend beyond transactional trades. The capacity to form and develop relationships becomes a pillar of their success, providing doors to opportunities that would otherwise be hidden.

Billionaires view innovation as a mindset rather than just an action. They consider innovation an essential component of their thought processes, and they are continuously on the lookout for new techniques and game-changing ideas. This mental tendency for innovation keeps them at the forefront of their industry, driving change rather than reacting to it.

In the long run, billionaires prioritize patience as a mental discipline. They retain a firm long-term perspective, realizing that long-term success is often the result of consistent effort over time. This mindset enables them to withstand short-term swings and setbacks, knowing that their vision is anchored in the distant horizon.

Billionaires understand the importance of managing their time and maximizing productivity. Their mentalities are finely designed to prioritize work, delegate effectively, and maximize productivity. This systematic approach to time management ensures that every moment is spent wisely, contributing to their total performance.

Billionaires prioritize philanthropy in addition to personal gain. Many people actively participate in philanthropy, seeing their riches as a tool for effecting positive change in the world. Giving back not only benefits society as a whole, but it also increases people's sense of fulfillment and purpose.

Unraveling billionaires' mentalities reveals that their achievement is not solely due to external circumstances or luck. Instead, it reflects deeply rooted thought patterns—a set of mental disciplines that propels them to excellence. As we investigate these mindsets, we discover not just the keys to financial success but also significant lessons in personal change that can be used by anybody looking to improve their life.

The Influence of Faith
The concept of faith has always been a powerful force in the human experience, transcending cultural, religious, and personal barriers. Its effect stretches far beyond the bounds of traditional spirituality, influencing the lives of those who have achieved great success, including some of the world's most well-known billionaires. In this investigation of "The 10 Habits of Billionaires: Powerful Lessons in Personal Change," we look at how faith has had a tremendous impact on the lives and

accomplishments of these extraordinary people.

Faith, at its core, is the steadfast belief in something more than oneself be it a higher force, a set of rules, or an innate feeling of purpose. Many billionaires credit their success not only to their abilities or acumen but also to an unwavering faith that helped them overcome obstacles and propel them toward their goals.

The power of vision is one aspect of faith that millionaires find particularly compelling. The ability to envisage victory and to look past the current difficulties and disappointments is a sign of faith. This practice adheres to the concept that the mind is capable of achieving anything it can imagine. Billionaires frequently talk about forming mental images of their goals and holding onto these ideas with unwavering faith, as if the act of visualizing propels them ahead on their route to success.

Furthermore, faith instills perseverance and persistence in billionaires. When conventional wisdom would tell you to give up in the face of hardship, faith drives an indomitable spirit that refuses to be defeated. It becomes the driving force that converts setbacks into stepping stones and failures into opportunities for advancement. Billionaires frequently credit their capacity to endure in the face of seemingly insurmountable problems to a deeply entrenched belief that there is a purpose to their undertakings, one that transcends beyond the immediate obstacles.

Faith has an impact on more than just personal belief; it also helps to foster meaningful relationships and a strong sense of belonging. Many billionaires express a sense of connectivity with the world around them, realizing that their success was not achieved alone but via collaboration and help from others. Faith, in this environment, becomes a unifying factor that promotes trust, cooperation, and a common goal for a better future.

Furthermore, faith acts as a guide for ethical decision-making. Billionaires who attribute their success to a deep faith frequently emphasize the value of integrity, honesty, and a commitment to doing good in the world. This moral compass, driven by faith, serves as the foundation upon which they construct their empires, ensuring that their activities are consistent with their ideals and favorably impact society.

Finally, faith's influence on billionaires' behaviors extends beyond a simple belief system; it becomes a driving force that determines their ideas, actions, and, ultimately, their destinies. Faith has a transformative effect on the lives of those who have achieved great success, whether via the power of vision, resilience in the face of adversity, the cultivation of meaningful relationships, or the guidance of ethical decision-making. As we negotiate the lessons of personal change, faith emerges as a powerful catalyst that propels individuals toward their goals, reminding us that the path to success is both material and spiritual.

A Mindset of Growth

In the labyrinth of success, where the path to riches and influence is frequently hidden by obstacles and uncertainty, one of the cardinal characteristics that distinguishes billionaires is their constant dedication to a growth mindset. An attitude that not only accepts but thrives on change, creating an environment conducive to invention, resilience, and unbounded success.

The path to a billionaire's mindset begins with acknowledging that growth is an ongoing process, an ever-changing voyage rather than a static destination. This realization is the foundation upon which the entire structure of success is built. Billionaires recognize that the world is constantly changing, and in order to traverse its dynamic currents, one must adopt a mindset that sees difficulties as stepping stones rather than barriers.

Embracing a growth mindset entails developing a strong sense of curiosity, an insatiable thirst for knowledge, and an unwavering willingness to learn from every event, whether triumph or loss. Billionaires recognize that true growth is found not just in gaining wealth but also in pushing the boundaries of their own intellectual and emotional capabilities. They become lifelong learners, constantly seeking new challenges and considering mistakes as great teachings in disguise.

This approach requires a willingness to venture outside of one's comfort zone. Billionaires understand that growth rarely happens within the confines of familiarity. Instead, they explore unexplored territory, confront the unknown, and embrace discomfort as a tool for personal and professional growth. This discomfort allows individuals to find their own dormant potential, unlocking new levels of creativity and perseverance.

Furthermore, a growth mindset is intrinsically linked to adaptability. Billionaires have an unprecedented ability to modify their plans, attitudes, and even long-held beliefs in reaction to changing circumstances. They recognize that rigidity is the enemy of progress and that flexibility is essential for not only surviving but also thriving in the ever-changing terrain of success.

The development of a growth mindset is not without hurdles. It necessitates a high level of self-awareness and the willingness to face one's own limitations. Billionaires appreciate the value of introspection and routinely analyze themselves to uncover areas for improvement. Setbacks are viewed as signs to rethink and recalibrate their approach, rather than indicators of personal failure.

To summarize, the growth mindset is a fundamental habit that underpins billionaires' success. It is a dedication to lifelong learning, embracing change, venturing outside of one's comfort zone, and adjusting to the ever-changing terrain of problems. Aspiring to mimic this mindset is more than just achieving financial success; it is also a journey toward inner transformation and a life of continuous expansion and fulfillment.

Sturdiness and adaptability

In the dynamic world of success, where fortunes rise and fall and industries experience fast shifts, the interplay between sturdiness and adaptability emerges as a pillar of billionaire behavior. Sturdiness serves as the basis upon which these industrial titans establish their empires, but adaptability enables them to manage the ever-changing tides of commerce. This delicate combination of resilience and adaptability is a crucial driver of billionaires' long-term success, providing significant insights into their attitude and approach to personal development.

In the context of billionaire habits, strength is connected with mental fortitude and unrelenting commitment. It is the ability to weather storms, confront adversity, and come out stronger on the other side. Billionaires recognize that setbacks are unavoidable, but it is their capacity to remain steady in the face of adversity that distinguishes them. They see problems as opportunities for growth and learning, rather than impenetrable barriers. The development of a strong attitude allows them to navigate the inevitable highs and lows of the entrepreneurial path with grace and perseverance.

Adaptability, on the other hand, is the secret weapon that enables millionaires to thrive in a constantly changing environment. The business scene is always changing, influenced by technical breakthroughs, market shifts, and global trends. Billionaires appreciate the importance of adapting their strategy, embracing change, and staying ahead of the curve. Their capacity to pivot, innovate, and reinvent themselves and their enterprises distinguishes them as leaders in their areas.

One cannot exist without the other—sturdiness and adaptability are inextricably linked in the billionaire's toolkit for success. Sturdiness serves as the anchor that keeps them grounded, whereas flexibility propels them ahead into unexplored territory. This delicate dance of toughness and flexibility results in a tremendous synergy that motivates their quest for greatness.

Billionaires frequently participate in mental toughness-enhancing treatments to enhance sturdiness. They actively work to reinforce their determination by using meditation, visualization, or establishing a growth mindset. They recognize the need for a solid foundation to survive the inevitable storms that come with every ambitious endeavor.

Billionaires understand the value of adaptation in the face of an ever-changing business landscape. They aggressively seek out new knowledge, stay current on developing trends, and surround themselves with varied viewpoints. This proactive approach allows them to pivot as needed, embrace emerging possibilities, and continuously innovate to stay ahead of the competition.

In the area of personal change, the combination of strength and adaptability becomes a guiding concept. Aspiring individuals might be inspired by these millionaire habits by understanding the need to develop mental resilience while keeping open to the possibilities that change presents. Individuals who adopt a strong and adaptive attitude are better able to overcome personal problems and seize opportunities for growth and change.

In essence, the union of strength and adaptability reveals the route to success, teaching essential lessons in personal development. Individuals who adopt these billionaire habits can strengthen their mental resilience, welcome change, and chart a course for long-term personal and professional fulfillment.

An Emphasis on Ongoing Education

In their tireless pursuit of success, billionaires have a similar thread that runs through the fabric of their amazing lives: an unshakable commitment to continued education. Beyond the gloss and glamour of their accomplishments lies a deep commitment to lifelong learning, a habit that distinguishes them on the route to money, influence, and personal growth.

The world is constantly evolving, with technological developments, commercial tactics, and global dynamics reshaping the environment at unprecedented rates. Billionaires understand that the key to managing this ever-changing environment is knowledge acquisition—a never-ending dedication to broadening their intellectual horizons.

One of the distinguishing characteristics of billionaires is their voracious curiosity. They see learning not as a means to a goal but as a lifetime adventure that broadens their perspective of the world and opens them to new opportunities. This voracious desire for information drives them to investigate a wide range of topics, including cutting-edge advances in their respective sectors as well as philosophy, science, and the arts.

Billionaires understand that education goes beyond formal institutions. While academic degrees are valuable, these industrial titans believe in a holistic approach to learning. They seek knowledge from a variety of sources, such as books, mentors, conferences, and networking events. In the digital age, they use online platforms, webinars, and podcasts to remain up-to-date on the newest trends and insights, displaying the adaptability required in today's fast-paced corporate environment.

Furthermore, billionaires understand that learning extends beyond success stories and achievements. They see failure as a powerful teacher, considering failures as useful lessons that motivate them to future success. This tenacity in the face of adversity demonstrates their dedication to continuous education—using every event, positive or unpleasant, as a springboard for personal improvement.

Billionaires' everyday routines include a strong emphasis on constant learning. They set aside time for reading, reflecting, and learning new skills. This proactive commitment to self-improvement enables them to stay ahead of the curve, anticipate industry trends, and make educated decisions that contribute to their long-term success.

Furthermore, millionaires understand the transformative power of sharing knowledge. Many of them actively participate in mentoring partnerships, passing on their wisdom to the next generation of ambitious entrepreneurs. They establish a learning culture within their enterprises, resulting in conditions that stimulate creativity and resourcefulness, ultimately contributing to the success of their initiatives.

Finally, a concentration on continual education is a key component of the habits that propel millionaires to greatness. These individuals stand out on their path to personal and professional achievement because they are committed to lifelong learning, have an insatiable curiosity, and are adaptable. Aspiring to replicate billionaires' habits can be a tremendous motivator for anyone looking for profound personal growth and unprecedented success.

Having an abundant and optimistic mindset

In the magnificent tapestry of prosperity weaved by billionaires, one recurring thread stands out prominently: an abundance and cheerful outlook. This chapter digs into the significant importance of building a mindset that loves wealth while simultaneously radiating optimism, revealing the secrets underlying these powerful behaviors that propel millionaires to amazing success.

The billionaire mindset is based on the steadfast idea that abundance is a limitless state of being rather than a finite resource. Billionaires recognize that the universe is endless and that people who approach life with an open heart and an abundance-oriented attitude have limitless potential. This perspective influences their judgments, behaviors, and reactions, resulting in a magnetic force that draws riches into their lives.

Optimism, the motivating factor behind this approach, is more than just a good attitude. It is often held that obstacles are opportunities disguised, and setbacks are stepping stones to greater success. Billionaires see the glass as more than half full; they see it as a never-ending source of opportunity. Their optimistic outlook enables them to face obstacles with resilience and inventiveness, transforming adversity into an advantage.

The habit of appreciation is an important part of creating an abundance mindset. Billionaires recognize the transformative impact of acknowledging and appreciating even the smallest benefits in their lives. Gratitude generates a positive feedback loop, generating more reasons to be grateful and cultivating a profound sense of contentment while pursuing ambitious goals.

Furthermore, billionaires actively practice visualization, a strong method by which they clearly imagine their intended goals. This technique not only establishes clear objectives but also connects their subconscious mind with the goals they want to achieve. Billionaires use visualization to use the law of attraction, attracting opportunities and resources that align with their desired level of success.

The willingness to take reasonable risks is an important part of an abundant mindset. Billionaires recognize that traveling into unexplored territory typically results in growth and innovation. Their optimism drives them to welcome uncertainty, considering it a blank canvas full of endless possibilities to be explored. This daring approach to risk-taking has been the foundation of many billionaires' careers, propelling them to unprecedented success.

To summarize, billionaires' bountiful and positive mindset is more than a habit; it is a way of life. This perspective defines their thoughts, influences their judgments, and propels their never-ending pursuit of greatness. As we peel back the layers of this strong habit, we learn that it is not reserved for the exceptional few but rather a transformative force available to anybody prepared to embrace life's limitless potential.

Taking Reasonably High Risks
Billionaires don't mind taking chances, as long as they do it carefully and strategically. They know that to succeed beyond their wildest dreams, they have to be prepared to take risks and venture beyond their comfort zones.

Billionaires, however, do not take unwarranted chances. They weigh the possible benefits and drawbacks carefully before deciding. Before acting, they get as much information as they can, speak with professionals, and consider the advantages and disadvantages.

An Emphasis on Long-Term Planning
Billionaires have a compelling and distinct future vision. They have a clear goal in mind and a plan of action for getting there. Even in the face of immediate obstacles, they remain committed to their goals and make decisions based on this long-term vision.

Billionaires are aware that success does not come easily. They are prepared to postpone happiness and make sacrifices in order to realize their long-term goals. They resist being quickly sidetracked or tempted, choosing instead to remain steadfast in their pursuit of their objectives and make steady progress toward them.

To sum up, the attitude of billionaires is defined by a strong sense of self-worth, a growth mindset, perseverance, resilience, a dedication to lifelong learning, an optimistic and abundant outlook, a readiness to take measured risks, and an emphasis on long-term goals. Readers may acquire the habits and thinking of billionaires and set themselves up for amazing success by embracing these mindset concepts.

The Value of Individual Growth

The secret to realizing your full potential and succeeding in all facets of your life is personal development. It's a never-ending path of personal development, maturation, and ongoing education. Personal development, as used in this book, is the deliberate and methodical process of creating the habits, abilities, and mentality necessary to become a billionaire.

Putting Yourself First

The idea that your biggest asset is yourself is one of the cornerstones of personal development. You have to invest in yourself first if you want to attain remarkable achievement. This entails making time, effort, and financial commitments to your own personal development. You need to invest in your own professional and personal development, just as millionaires do in their companies and financial endeavors.

You can invest in yourself in a variety of ways. It could entail going to seminars, attending workshops, finding mentors and role models who can mentor and inspire you, or taking part in personal development activities like reading, visiting workshops, or attending seminars in order to gain new knowledge and abilities. Investing in yourself gives you the knowledge and resources you need to take advantage of the possibilities and challenges life presents.

Gaining Awareness of Oneself

A vital element of personal growth is self-awareness. It entails comprehending your motives, values, beliefs, and areas of strength and weakness. Gaining self-awareness helps you understand yourself better and learn how to take advantage of your advantages over disadvantages in order to accomplish your objectives.

Being self-aware also enables you to see your areas of strength and development. Empowering you to make positive changes helps you identify thoughts or behavior patterns that might be preventing you from moving forward. You can make deliberate decisions that support your objectives and core beliefs by being cognizant of your thoughts, feelings, and behaviors.

Having Specific Objectives

Establishing goals is a crucial part of personal growth. It is difficult to move forward and assess your progress in the absence of specific goals. Billionaires know how important it is to have precise, attainable goals. They are aware that objectives give drive, direction, and focus.

Make sure your goals are in line with your values and aspirations when you set them. They should be realistic and reachable, yet just difficult enough to force you outside of your comfort zone. You may boost your chances of success and build a roadmap for your personal growth journey by defining specific goals.

Ongoing Education and Development

Wealthy people are perpetual learners. They are aware that information is power and that continuing education is crucial for both professional and personal development. They never stop looking for fresh data, viewpoints, and insights to broaden their horizons and keep on top of things.

In order to develop a development mentality and attain achievement comparable to that of a billionaire, you need to take a similar approach to education. This entails having an open mind, viewing obstacles as chances for personal development, and actively seeking out educational opportunities in all spheres of your life. Every learning opportunity, whether it's from reading books, going to seminars, taking courses, or having in-depth conversations, can advance your personal development.

Fostering Adaptability and Resilience

Acquiring information and skills is only one aspect of personal development; another is building the resilience and adaptability required to deal with life's ups and downs. Billionaires are aware that failure and setbacks are a necessary part of the journey to success. They see these difficulties as chances for growth and use them to become stronger and more resilient.

Developing a growth mindset is essential to building resilience. This entails accepting challenges, reinterpreting setbacks as teaching moments, and persevering in the face of difficulties. It also calls for the development of emotional intelligence, which is the capacity to recognize and control your emotions, as well as the creation of solid support systems that can offer direction and encouragement in trying circumstances.

Juggling Personal and Work Life

The goal of personal development is to achieve holistic success in all facets of your life, not just financial achievement. Billionaires know how important it is to keep a healthy balance between their personal and work lives. They place equal importance on their work endeavors and their relationships, health, and general well-being.

Establishing healthy routines and boundaries is essential to achieving overall success. This entails giving self-care first priority, preserving deep connections, and scheduling time for pursuits that make you happy and fulfilled. Finding a balance between your personal and professional lives will help you remain successful and happy in the long run.

Accepting Personal Development as a Path

Personal development is a lifelong journey rather than a destination. It calls for a dedication to ongoing learning, development, and progress. Billionaires know that personal growth is a process that takes time, effort, and commitment; it is not something that can be accomplished quickly.

It's crucial to enjoy the process and the advancements you make as you set out on your personal growth path. No matter how minor, acknowledge your accomplishments and take lessons from your mistakes. Recall that becoming the best version of yourself and making progress are the goals of personal growth rather than perfection.

To sum up, developing oneself is the first step toward becoming a billionaire. You can realize your greatest potential and design an abundant and fulfilling life by making an investment in yourself, growing in self-awareness, establishing clear goals, learning and growing constantly, building resilience, striking a balance between your personal and professional lives, and accepting personal growth as a lifelong journey. Your personal growth path will be guided by the routines and habits in this book, which will enable you to succeed extraordinarily in all aspects of your life.

The Path to Achievement

Achieving success is a journey rather than a destination. It's a road that calls for commitment, tenacity, and an openness to change. This chapter will examine the path to success and the essential components that can support you in realizing your ambitions.

Accepting Adaptation

Being open to change is the first step on the path to success. It is inevitable that change will occur, and those who oppose it frequently find themselves unable to advance and locked in one spot. People who are successful recognize that change is essential for personal development and are receptive to fresh insights, viewpoints, and chances.

You have to evaluate where you are now and what needs to change before you can start along the path to success. This can entail reassessing your routines, perspective, or even your objectives. It takes a different perspective, the courage to push yourself beyond your comfort zone, and a dedication to personal development to embrace change.

Clearly Determining Your Objectives

Setting specific goals is the next stage on your path to success after you have accepted change. Setting goals gives you focus and direction, as well as something to work toward. Without specific objectives, it is easy to get sidetracked or lose motivation.

SMART is for specified, measurable, achievable, relevant, and time-bound, and this is a crucial consideration while making goals. This guarantees that your objectives are doable and practical. Your larger objectives can be broken down into more achievable activities, and this will help you to build a successful road map.

Acting

Achieving your goals requires action; setting goals is only the first step. People who are successful recognize the value of acting consistently and deliberately to achieve their objectives. They take initiative and create their own opportunities, rather than waiting for them to present themselves.

Prioritize your tasks and create a plan before you can take action. This entails determining the most crucial and significant steps that will advance your objectives. It also calls for perseverance and discipline in carrying out your goal in the face of obstacles or failures.

Getting Past Challenges

There are challenges on the path to success. Obstacles and disappointments are unavoidable, but how you handle them will ultimately define your level of success. Successful people see challenges as chances for development and education. They are tenacious and resilient in the face of difficulty.

It is crucial to cultivate a growth mentality in order to overcome challenges. This entails redefining obstacles as chances for development and learning. It also calls for the growth of emotional intelligence as well as the capacity for good stress and failure management. Through perseverance, flexibility, and attention, you can overcome setbacks and carry on with your successful journey.

Marking Important Occasions

It's critical to recognize your advancement and appreciate small victories along the way to success. Celebrating accomplishments gives you a boost in confidence and drive while also letting you take stock of your progress. It serves as a reminder that success involves more than simply achieving your ultimate objective; it also involves the development and accomplishments you have along the way.

It is important to recognize and commemorate your accomplishments, regardless of how minor they may appear. This will encourage you to keep moving forward and boost your motivation. Recall that achieving your goals requires a journey, with each milestone serving as a springboard.

Looking for Guidance and Assistance

Without the help and direction of others, no successful trip can be considered complete. People who are successful know how important it is to surround themselves with people who share their values and who can offer guidance, support, and mentorship. They look for role models who have attained their goals so they can pick up tips from them.

Along the way, seeking out mentoring and assistance can offer insightful advice, accountability, and direction. You can overcome obstacles, steer clear of typical hazards, and advance more quickly with its assistance. Embrace a support system of people who can assist you in achieving your objectives and who share your vision.

Ongoing Education and Development

Achieving success is a lifelong process rather than a single event. People who are successful recognize the value of lifelong learning and development. They invest in learning new information, abilities, and viewpoints because they are dedicated to their own personal growth.

Making learning a priority in your life can help you keep growing. Take classes, go to seminars, read books, and look for new experiences. Adopt a growth mentality and keep an open mind to fresh viewpoints. You can stay ahead of the curve and adjust to the ever-changing terrain of success by never stopping learning and developing.

Savoring the Trip

Lastly, don't forget to enjoy the trip. Achieving success involves more than just finishing the task at hand; it also involves the growth, learning, and experiences you have along the way. Savor the little wins, rejoice at the big ones, and embrace the challenges.

Give yourself some time to reflect on your accomplishments and the person you are growing into. Savor the journey of self-improvement and the sense of accomplishment that arises from following your interests and goals. Success is a lifetime journey of self-discovery and personal fulfillment, rather than just a destination.

In summary, achieving success is a life-changing and empowering experience. You can start down a path that leads to amazing success by accepting change, defining clear goals, acting, getting past hurdles, celebrating victories, asking for help, and never stopping learning and developing. Recall that success is all about the journey, not simply the end point. Savor the growth along the road, accept the challenges, and enjoy the process.

MASTERING TIME MANAGEMENT

Clearly Determining Objectives

One essential habit that millionaires have learned to perfect in order to attain amazing success is setting clear goals. Without well-defined objectives, achieving desired results and navigating the route to success become challenging. This section will discuss the value of having specific goals and offer readers doable tactics they may use in their own lives.

The Influence of Establishing Objectives

Setting goals is an effective technique that enables people to identify their objectives and design a plan of action to reach them. Billionaires know how important it is to have specific goals because it gives them drive, direction, and focus. When objectives are well-defined, they serve as a catalyst for motivation and inspiration, encouraging people to act and advance.

Setting and following clear goals aids in work prioritization and decision-making. People are better able to coordinate their actions and efforts when they have a clear vision of what they want to accomplish. As a result, they are able to make decisions that are consistent with their objectives and steer clear of distractions and needless side trips.

Techniques for Clearly Defined Goals

Describe your goals: Start by imagining the future you want. What goals do you have in mind? For you, what does success look like? Spend some time thinking back on your dreams and visualizing your objectives clearly. This will act as the cornerstone for establishing precise and significant objectives.

Be Specific: It's hard to measure and accomplish vague goals. Establish clear objectives by making them precise and well-defined. Don't just say, "I want to be successful," but rather, explain what success means to you. For instance, "I want to start my own business and generate $1 million in revenue within five years."

Establish Measurable Milestones: Divide your objectives into more manageable, quantifiable benchmarks. This enables you to monitor your development and recognize your accomplishments as you go. If your objective is to lose weight, for example, create benchmarks like 5 pounds lost in the first month, 10 pounds lost in the second, and so forth.

Make Your Goals Achievable: Although having lofty objectives is vital, your goals should also be reachable. Impossible ambitions can cause demotivation and frustration. When setting objectives, take into account your available resources, abilities, and situation to make sure they are doable.

Establish a Timeline: To foster a sense of urgency and accountability, give each goal a deadline. Setting deadlines aids in task prioritization and concentration. Divide your objectives into three categories: short-, medium-, and long-term, and give each a reasonable deadline.

Put Your Goals in Writing: Studies have indicated that putting goals in writing enhances the chance of accomplishing them. You commit to yourself and provide yourself with a concrete reminder of your objectives when you put your goals in writing. Your written goals should be kept in plain sight to act as a continual reminder.

Review and Modify: Evaluate your progress and goals on a regular basis. You might need to modify your goals in order to keep them in line with your changing aspirations as you gain new insights and experiences. Remain flexible and willing to modify your objectives as needed.

Putting Goal-Setting into Practice in Your Life
It's now time to put goal-setting into practice in your own life since you know how important it is to have specific goals and you have tools to help you along the way. To get you started, follow these steps:

Think About Your Goals: Set aside some time to consider your long-term goals and what you hope to accomplish in a variety of spheres of your life, including work, relationships, health, and personal growth.

Establish Your Objectives: Using the previously discussed

methodologies, establish your objectives based on your reflections. Ensure that they are SMART goals—specific, measurable, attainable, relevant, and time-bound.

Make an action plan by dividing your objectives into manageable chunks. Determine the assignments and deadlines that will help you reach your objectives. You'll be able to stay organized and progress-focused by doing this.

Monitor Your Progress: Continually reevaluate your objectives and monitor your advancement. Honor your accomplishments and make the necessary corrections. To hold yourself accountable, use resources like notebooks or goal-tracking applications.

Remind yourself of the reasons you set your goals in the first place and keep them in plain sight to stay motivated. As you progress, surround yourself with positive, like-minded people who can inspire and drive you.

Recall that defining specific objectives is only the first step. It's critical to act consistently and maintain your commitment to your objectives. You can find success in life and do remarkable things if you have a clear vision and a well-defined plan.

Setting Task Priorities
Within the rapidly evolving and fiercely competitive realm of

billionaires, time is an invaluable asset. They are aware that setting priorities for work will help them reach their objectives and be as productive as possible. Setting priorities involves more than just finishing duties; it also involves concentrating on the most significant and lasting projects that support the organization's long-term goals and vision. This section will examine the methods and approaches employed by billionaires to efficiently choose priorities and maximize their available time.

The Matrix of Eisenhower

The Eisenhower Matrix is a common tool used by billionaires to prioritize their work. This matrix aids people in classifying jobs according to their significance and urgency. There are four quadrants in it:

Important and Urgent: Activities in this quadrant are crucial to achieving goals and call for quick attention. Billionaires give these jobs top priority and deal with them initially to avoid any future emergencies or lost opportunities.

Important but Not Urgent: Although they don't need to be completed right now, the tasks in this quadrant are essential for long-term success. Billionaires set aside specific time to work on these projects, making sure they are not overlooked or eclipsed by more pressing issues.

Urgent but Not Important: Although the tasks in this quadrant appear urgent, they don't make a big difference toward their long-term objectives. When it's feasible, billionaires assign these chores to others or do away with them entirely to free up time for more crucial pursuits.

Tasks in this quadrant are low priority and do not meet their objectives since they are neither urgent nor important. Billionaires steer clear of these activities completely because they might be sources of distraction that impede development.

Billionaires are able to efficiently prioritize and choose where to focus their time and energy by applying the Eisenhower Matrix to rapidly evaluate the significance and urgency of their work.

Matching Objectives with Tasks

Billionaires know how important it is to match tasks to long-term objectives. They make sure that every task they take on advances their well-defined vision of what they want to accomplish. They assess whether the tasks they are working on are bringing them closer to their desired results on a regular basis, and they reevaluate their goals.

Billionaires pose the following queries to themselves in order to properly prioritize tasks:

Does this assignment support my long-term objectives?
Will my success be significantly impacted by finishing this task?
Is it possible to assign or remove this task?
What might happen if you don't finish this assignment?
Billionaires are able to make well-informed decisions on which tasks to prioritize, assign, or eliminate by continuously comparing them to their goals. By using this strategy, they may be sure that their time and efforts are being directed toward tasks that will help them achieve their goals.

Blocking Time

Another tactic used by billionaires to efficiently manage their time and prioritize work is time blocking. They set up particular time blocks for various tasks, making sure to give each one their full attention and focus. Billionaires can boost productivity and minimize distractions by dedicating dedicated time to critical tasks.

Billionaires frequently plan their most significant and difficult tasks for when they are most focused and energized. They are aware that during the day, their physical and mental energy levels change, and they may maximize their performance by matching their tasks to their energy levels.

Billionaires also assign themselves tasks with reasonable due dates and hold themselves responsible for completing them on time. They are aware of how crucial consistency and discipline are to reaching their objectives, and they make sure that things are finished on schedule by sticking to their time slots.

Consistent Assessment and Modification
Setting priorities for tasks is a continuous process that needs to be reviewed and adjusted on a regular basis. Billionaires are aware that things change and that there can be new projects and objectives to consider. They reevaluate their objectives, look over their to-do lists, and rearrange their priorities as needed on a frequent basis.

Billionaires constantly work on the most significant and influential tasks by periodically assessing and rearranging their task priorities. They are adaptive and versatile, ready to change course when fresh chances or difficulties present themselves.

To sum up, billionaires have learned the critical talent of prioritizing tasks in order to maximize their productivity and accomplish their objectives. Billionaires make sure their time and energy are directed toward things that will help them achieve their goals by employing methods such as the Eisenhower Matrix, time blocking, goal alignment, and frequent assessment and reordering of tasks. Readers can increase their productivity and make great strides toward their personal objectives by implementing these tactics.

Get Rid of Time Wasters
Time is a valuable resource, particularly for millionaires who recognize the importance of each and every second. This chapter will discuss the value of getting rid of time waste and how

doing so can greatly increase your success and productivity. You may recover time and use it toward more worthwhile endeavors by recognizing and removing activities that don't advance your objectives.

Recognizing Inefficient People

Finding time wasters is the first step in getting rid of them. Activities that take up your time but don't add much value or advance your objectives are called time wasters. They can be internal or external elements that reduce productivity. Among the frequent time-wasters are:

Delaying

The act of putting off or delaying necessary duties is known as procrastination. It frequently results from feeling overburdened, lacking enthusiasm, or fearing failure. Since procrastination keeps you from moving forward and accomplishing your objectives, it may be a major time waste.

Overuse of social media Make use of

Social media sites have the potential to become highly addictive and quickly take up a lot of your time. While viewing movies, participating in online chats, and mindlessly browsing through feeds can be entertaining, they can also be significant distractions that reduce productivity.

Extraneous Gatherings

Meetings can be a great way to collaborate and make decisions, but they can also take up a lot of time. A lot of meetings are ineffective because they lack a defined goal or agenda. Attending meetings that don't advance your objectives can cost you time that could be better used on other, more crucial projects.

Taking on multiple tasks at once

It's a common misconception that multitasking boosts productivity. It can actually be a huge time-waster. Attempting to balance several activities at once divides your focus and attention, which lowers productivity and lowers the caliber of your work. It is preferable to concentrate entirely on one task at a time.

Techniques for Getting Rid of Time Wasters

After identifying a few typical time wasters, let's look at ways to get rid of them from your regular routine. You will be able to better manage and recover your time by putting these strategies into practice.

Set task priorities.
Setting priorities for your work is one of the best strategies to get rid of time wasters. Determine which of your duties are the most critical and pressing, then concentrate on finishing them first. You can make sure that the things you are putting your time towards are the most important and in line with your objectives by setting priorities for your work.

Define your boundaries.
Eliminating time waste requires setting clear boundaries. Acquire the ability to decline engagements and activities that conflict with your principles or aspirations. You can safeguard your time and energy and concentrate on what is really important by establishing boundaries.

Assign and Contract
Your time is precious as a billionaire, so it's critical to assign jobs that can be completed by others. Determine which jobs can be assigned to someone else or outsourced in order to free up time for more crucial duties. By delegating, you can take advantage of other people's abilities and knowledge while simultaneously getting rid of time wasters.

Put time-blocking into practice.
Using the time-blocking strategy, you set up particular time slots for various projects or pursuits. By planning your day and allocating particular timeslots for various tasks, you establish a framework that aids in maintaining concentration and

preventing interruptions. By ensuring that you are allocating your time to tasks that support your objectives, time blocking enables you to get rid of time wasters.

Cut Down on Diversions
Distractions can seriously lower your output and cause you to lose important time. Recognize and reduce distractions around you. This can entail blocking distracting websites and apps using productivity tools, setting up a designated workstation, or turning off phone notifications. You can establish an environment that encourages focus and productivity by reducing distractions.

Developing Time Management Techniques
Removing time wasters is a continuous activity rather than a one-time event. It calls for developing successful time management techniques that boost your output and achievement. The following routines can assist you in getting rid of time wasters and optimizing your time:

Organize your day.
Make a strategy for your daily responsibilities and activities before you begin. Prioritize your work according to its urgency and importance, and set clear targets. Having a strategy helps you stay on task and prevents you from getting distracted by unproductive activities.

Develop your sense of time.
Effective time management requires developing a sense of time awareness. Keep an eye on how you spend your time and look for any trends in the things you do that waste it. You can eliminate time wasters and refocus your attention on more productive work by making conscious decisions based on your awareness of how you utilize your time.

Periodically assess and modify
Make it a habit to review your time management and determine whether any particular activity is worthwhile. Be prepared to modify your plans and cut out anything that doesn't help you

achieve your objectives. You may increase your productivity by reviewing and improving your time management techniques on a regular basis.

Acquire the ability to say no.
Saying no is a strong ability that can assist you in getting rid of time wasters. Choose carefully whatever obligations and pursuits you participate in. Have the guts to turn down an opportunity or request if it does not fit with your values or aspirations. Saying no to unimportant things makes room for more worthwhile and fruitful endeavors.

Put mindfulness into practice.
Being totally present and involved in the present moment is the practice of mindfulness. You may increase your awareness of how you spend your time and make deliberate decisions to get rid of time wasters by practicing mindfulness. Additionally, mindfulness aids in maintaining attention and preventing distractions.

A vital first step in increasing your productivity and accomplishing your objectives is getting rid of time wasters. You may recover valuable time and allocate it to activities that support your goals by recognizing and removing those that don't help you succeed. Recall that time is a limited resource, and your decision about how to use it will determine how successful you are in becoming a millionaire.

Designing Effective Systems

One essential quality of successful people and billionaires is efficiency. They are aware that in order to maximize output and outcomes, they must optimize their time, resources, and procedures. This section will discuss the idea of designing effective systems and how it can help you succeed.

Simplifying Procedures

Streamlining workflows is a crucial component of developing effective systems. Since time is a scarce resource, billionaires try to streamline their work processes by getting rid of pointless procedures and inefficiencies. They examine their processes to find areas that could use improvement.

Start by outlining your present procedures if you want to optimize your workflows. Determine if there are any repetitive jobs, bottlenecks, or redundancies. To free up time for more vital activities, look for ways to automate or assign some jobs. By streamlining your processes, you may operate more efficiently and complete more tasks in less time.

Making Use of Technology

Technology is essential to the development of effective systems. Billionaires use technology to collect data for well-informed decision-making, automate monotonous jobs, and improve communication. They keep up with the newest hardware and software available, which can improve their output and effectiveness.

Examine your present IT setup and pinpoint places where you may use technology to increase productivity. To improve efficiency, think about integrating automation software, communication tools, and project management software. Using technology to its full potential will save you time, cut down on mistakes, and enhance teamwork.

Outsourcing and Delegation

One thing that billionaires are good at is delegation. They know they can't do it all alone and that giving jobs to competent people can free up their time for more strategic endeavors. They can concentrate on high-value tasks that enhance their overall performance by delegating well.

Assess the amount of work you are doing and decide which duties you can assign to others. Seek out people on your team or think about contracting out some work to outside experts. Trust, good training, and open communication are necessary for effective delegation. You may establish more effective processes and make sure your time is spent on things that support your priorities and goals by assigning duties to others.

Ongoing Enhancement

Developing effective systems is a continuous effort. Billionaires frequently assess their systems to find opportunities for improvement because they recognize the value of continual improvement. To make sure that their processes continue to be successful and efficient, they ask for input from their staff, examine data, and keep up with market developments.

Examine your systems and procedures on a regular basis to find areas that could use improvement. Invite team members to provide feedback and be receptive to suggestions for improvement. Adopt a philosophy of constant improvement and show a willingness to modify and advance your systems as necessary. You can maintain a high level of efficiency and stay ahead of the competition by continuously improving your systems.

Removing Interruptions

Distractions can seriously impair efficiency and production. Billionaires know how important it is to stay focused and remove distractions from their workspace. They design procedures and tactics to reduce distractions and increase their focus on crucial work.

Examine your workspace and note any possible distractions. This can include electronic distractions like social media notifications, noise, and clutter. Take action to reduce or get rid of these distractions. To keep concentration and boost productivity, designate a specific area for work, set limits with coworkers or family members, and apply productivity strategies like time blocking or the Pomodoro Technique.

Process Standardization

Creating efficient systems also requires standardizing processes. Billionaires understand the importance of repeatability and consistency in their business practices. They provide guidelines and standard operating procedures to guarantee that jobs are carried out successfully and efficiently.

Examine your present procedures and pinpoint areas that could benefit from uniformity. Create checklists or templates to expedite workflows, provide criteria for decision-making, and develop clear and simple procedures for repetitive tasks. Process standardization may lower errors, boost productivity, and lay the groundwork for future expansion and scalability.

Tracking and Assessing Results

You must test and monitor performance if you want to make sure that your systems are working effectively. Billionaires monitor key performance indicators (KPIs) to assess how well their systems are working and pinpoint areas that need work. They optimize their processes and make well-informed decisions by utilizing data-driven insights.

Determine which KPIs are pertinent to your company's or personal objectives. Metrics like productivity, turnaround time, customer happiness, or revenue growth may be included in this. Put in place mechanisms for routinely monitoring and assessing these KPIs. Determine patterns, regions for development, and chances for optimization by analyzing the data. You can continuously increase your productivity and make data-driven decisions by tracking and evaluating performance.

Making Training and Development Invested

Understanding and experience are necessary to create effective systems. Billionaires know how important it is to put money into their own and their teams' professional growth. To be at the forefront of their industry, they are always looking for ways to improve their knowledge and abilities.

Determine the areas that could use more training or growth for you or your team. These could be knowledge unique to the industry, leadership abilities, or technical capabilities. Set aside time and resources for workshops, online courses, and training initiatives. Through training and development, you can acquire the abilities and know-how required to design and manage effective systems.

A key component of success is the development of effective systems. A foundation for increased productivity, effectiveness, and success can be built by streamlining workflows, utilizing technology, delegating effectively, improving continuously, getting rid of distractions, standardizing procedures, keeping an eye on performance, and making training and development investments. Adopt an efficient mindset and give it top importance in both your personal and professional lives.

CULTIVATING RESILIENCE

3.1 Viewing Setbacks as a Chance for Growth

Failure is frequently viewed as an undesirable result that should be avoided at all costs. Nonetheless, failure is not something to be feared but rather welcomed as an invaluable learning experience for billionaires and other extremely successful people. In this section, we'll look at how millionaires take use of failure and why accepting failure is essential for personal development.

The Ability to Fail
Even billionaires have faced their fair share of failures and disappointments; failure is an essential part of life. But their ability to see failure as a springboard rather than an impediment to success is what makes them unique. They know that failing does not mean they are less good or incapable; rather, it means they have an opportunity to develop and learn.

Billionaires who accept failure can do the following:

Acquire knowledge through errors.
Lessons from failure that come from success alone are invaluable. Billionaires, when things don't work out as they had hoped, take the time to analyze what went wrong and pinpoint the reasons for their failure. They examine what went wrong, draw lessons from it, and apply that understanding to future decision-making.

Build your resilience.
Even though failure can be emotionally taxing, millionaires have learned to be resilient enough to overcome setbacks. They realize that a momentary setback on the road to success does not signify failure as the end. They develop the willpower and mental toughness required to endure in the face of difficulty by accepting failure.

Encourage innovation and creativity
Failure frequently pushes people to look creatively and unconventionally for solutions. Billionaires use their imagination and creative problem-solving skills to come up with other solutions when faced with failure. In their eyes, failure is a

chance to go against the grain and discover new things.

Making Success Out of Failure

Billionaires know how to turn their setbacks into successes, therefore accepting defeat is not enough. They employ the following tactics:

Consider and Analyze

Billionaires, when faced with failure, pause to consider what went wrong and examine it. They seek out frank feedback and pose difficult questions to themselves. They can avoid making the same mistakes again by identifying the underlying reasons behind their failure and making the required corrections.

Adapt and modify

Billionaires know that when they fail, it's usually necessary to modify their plans and find new ways to succeed. If it means accomplishing their objectives, they don't hesitate to alter their strategy or direction. To improve their chances of success, they view failure as a time to reevaluate their strategies and make the required changes.

Hold on and remain inspired.

While it can be disheartening to fail, billionaires have the fortitude to keep going when things get hard. They stay upbeat and concentrate on their long-term goal. They are aware that perseverance and determination are necessary for success and that failure is only a temporary setback.

Seek Assistance and Take Input from Others

Billionaires understand the value of consulting with others and getting advice. They envelop themselves in a network of like-minded people, mentors, and advisors who can offer direction and encouragement when things become tough. They are aware that failure is something that cannot be handled alone and that getting advice and insight from others may be very helpful in conquering challenges.

Accepting Failure in Your Personal Life

Anyone may adopt the mindset of accepting failure as a teaching opportunity; it's not just for billionaires. You can accept failure and turn it to your advantage by following these steps:

Modify your viewpoint
Reframe your failure-related perspective. Consider it an opportunity to develop and learn, as opposed to a bad consequence. Recognize that failing is not a reflection on your value but rather a chance to grow.

Think and Acquire Knowledge
When you go through a period of failure, consider what went wrong and what you may learn from it. Be truthful with yourself and ask for other people's opinions. Make smarter selections using this knowledge to enhance your future results.

Remain Fortitude
Gain the capacity to withstand setbacks and recover from them. Recognize that obstacles are inevitable on the path to success and that perseverance is essential. Remain optimistic, remain driven, and focus on your long-term goals.

Seek Assistance
Encircle yourself with a network of mentors, advisors, and like-minded people who can offer support and direction when things get tough. When faced with failure, take advice from them and learn from their experiences.

Take Measures
Accepting failure as a part of life does not mean that you can't move past it and use it to your advantage. Examine your shortcomings, make the required corrections, and modify your approach. Stick with it and don't give up on your objectives when things get hard.

You can realize your full potential and attain amazing success by accepting failure as a teaching opportunity. Recall that failure is only a roadblock on the way to greatness; it is not the end.

3.2 Creating a Growth Mentality

Developing a growth mentality is one of the most important habits that millionaires have developed in their pursuit of success. The idea that skills and intelligence can be developed through commitment, effort, and a desire to learn is known as a growth mindset. People with this mentality may rise to challenges, keep going in the face of setbacks, and never stop looking for ways to get better.

3.2.1 Accepting Difficulties and Educational Possibilities

Billionaires know that obstacles are only chances for development rather than impediments. They welcome obstacles as opportunities to grow intellectually, acquire new abilities, and learn. Rather than running from challenging circumstances, they confront them with curiosity and a will to succeed.

Billionaires push themselves beyond their comfort zones and uncover new abilities they never knew they had by accepting difficulties. They realize that failure is a necessary step toward achievement rather than a reflection of their value. They see failures as important teaching opportunities that offer perceptions and guidance for subsequent undertakings.

3.2.2 Taking a Positive Viewpoint

One of the main elements of a growth mentality is optimism. Billionaires are aware of the impact that positive thinking may have on their behavior and results. They choose to concentrate on finding answers rather than wallowing in issues, and they remain upbeat despite hardship.

Billionaires are resilient and determined when faced with adversity because they have an optimistic outlook. They think they are capable of solving issues in novel ways and overcoming any challenge. Their ability to maintain motivation and perseverance in the face of adversity ultimately results in increased achievement.

3.2.3 Keeping Going Despite Setbacks
One characteristic of a growth mentality is persistence. Billionaires know that hard work and hurdles are usually necessary for success. Even in the face of difficulties and disappointments, they are prepared to invest the time and effort required to accomplish their objectives.

Billionaires don't give up easily when faced with challenges. They see obstacles as transient hurdles that may be cleared with tenacity and resolve. They are prepared to modify their tactics, ask mentors for guidance, and absorb failures as lessons in order to discover different avenues for achievement.

3.2.4 Ongoing Education and Development
Billionaires are committed to lifelong learning and have a voracious appetite for knowledge. They are aware that success and personal development are continual processes rather than static ones. They actively look for chances to pick up new skills and broaden their knowledge in different fields.

Billionaires remain ahead of the curve and adjust to changing conditions by never stopping to learn and grow. They make an investment in their own growth—whether it's by reading books, going to seminars, or asking mentors for advice. They are able to remain creative, make wise decisions, and take advantage of new chances because of their dedication to learning.

Gaining a growth mentality takes time to develop. It calls for commitment, introspection, and a readiness to confront one's own assumptions and constraints. Nonetheless, people can realize their full potential and experience remarkable success in all facets of life by embracing a growth mentality.

In the next part, we will discuss the value of developing emotional intelligence and how it helps cultivate a growth mindset.

3.3 Developing the Emotional Capacity

One key characteristic that separates millionaires from the rest is emotional intelligence. It is the capacity to identify, comprehend, and control both our own and other people's feelings. Developing emotional intelligence makes it possible for millionaires to make wise decisions, overcome challenging circumstances, and forge solid connections. This section will discuss the value of emotional intelligence and offer doable methods for honing this crucial ability.

Emotional Intelligence's Power

It's common to refer to emotional intelligence as the "X-factor" that sets successful people apart from regular people. Beyond mere intellect and technical proficiency, it includes empathy, self-awareness, and proficient communication. Billionaires are aware of the important role emotions play in making decisions, solving problems, and forming deep connections.

Billionaires who have developed their emotional intelligence are better able to manage stress, adjust to change, and motivate others. They are very aware of and skilled at controlling their own emotions, which enables them to maintain composure and make thoughtful choices under duress. They also have the capacity for empathy, which helps them form enduring bonds with people and have an impact on those around them.

Growing in Self-Awareness

The cornerstone of emotional intelligence is self-awareness. It entails being aware of our own feelings, virtues, flaws, and emotions. Introspection and self-reflection are priorities for billionaires in order to have a profound insight into themselves. They evaluate their feelings, ideas, and actions on a frequent basis in order to spot trends and areas that need work.

Mindfulness is a vital discipline for developing self-awareness. Being mindful entails paying close attention to the here and now and objectively assessing our feelings and ideas. Billionaires frequently include journaling or meditation in their daily routines as mindfulness exercises. By increasing their awareness of their feelings and mental processes, these exercises enable kids to respond to difficult circumstances rather than just react to them.

Developing Compassion
The capacity to comprehend and feel another person's emotions is known as empathy. Billionaires understand the value of empathy in establishing trusting bonds and encouraging teamwork. They genuinely care about the welfare of those around them, actively listen to others, and make an effort to comprehend diverse viewpoints.

Active listening is a skill that millionaires use to develop empathy. They keep eye contact, focus entirely on the other person, and pose open-ended inquiries to elicit more in-depth dialogue. They also try to imagine themselves in other people's situations, taking into account their feelings and past experiences. Billionaires are able to establish rapport, trust, and a deeper connection with people by cultivating empathy.

Controlling your emotions
Being emotionally intelligent means knowing how to control our own feelings. Billionaires have learned to control their emotions in order to make logical decisions because they recognize that emotions may be strong motivators of behavior. They've learned coping mechanisms for handling pressure, overcoming obstacles, and keeping an optimistic outlook.

Reframing is one method billionaires use to control their

emotions. They make the deliberate decision to see obstacles as chances for development and education. They put more effort into coming up with answers and making proactive moves toward their objectives than they do into moping over unpleasant feelings. They also exercise, spend time in nature, or pursue hobbies as forms of self-care. These activities aid in their relaxation and renewal.

Developing robust connections

A crucial component of emotional intelligence is the ability to form solid relationships. Billionaires know that cooperation and teamwork are crucial for success and that individual achievement is not possible. They devote time and energy to developing connections with mentors, coworkers, and other powerful people.

Effective communication is a priority for billionaires in order to build deep bonds with others. They are adept at assertively and clearly expressing their feelings and opinions. In an effort to comprehend the needs and viewpoints of others, they also actively listen to them. Billionaires build an atmosphere of trust and respect through encouraging candid and open communication, which strengthens bonds and promotes teamwork.

In summary

Developing emotional intelligence is essential to succeeding in life and finding fulfillment. Billionaires have developed their emotional intelligence to overcome obstacles, form enduring bonds with others, and make wise choices. Through the processes of self-awareness, empathy cultivation, emotion management, and strong relationship development, readers can fully realize their potential and improve their emotional intelligence. We will discuss the value of stress management and self-care techniques in the next part as they relate to achieving success.

3.4 Putting Stress Management and Self-Care into Practice
Self-care and stress management are often neglected in the hectic and demanding world of billionaires. But these habits are essential to preserving long-term success and leading a balanced, healthy life. This section will discuss the value of stress management and self-care for billionaires and offer doable methods for adopting these practices in your own life.

The value of personal care
Billionaires know that looking after themselves is essential rather than a luxury. They understand that being in good physical, mental, and emotional health directly affects their capacity to give their best work and make wise judgments. Self-care is an investment in oneself that benefits one's entire life; it is not selfishness.

Putting physical health first
Billionaires place a high priority on maintaining good physical health through consistent exercise, a balanced diet, and adequate sleep. They know that physical vitality is necessary for long-term success and that a healthy body is the cornerstone of a healthy mind. Billionaires make sure they have the strength and energy to face any obstacles by scheduling regular exercise, eating a balanced diet, and getting enough sleep.

Taking Care of Your Mental and Emotional Health
Billionaires value not just their physical health but also their mental and emotional health. They know how important it is to take care of their thoughts, develop happy feelings, and manage stress. Billionaires frequently use writing, mindfulness exercises, and meditation to improve attention, lower stress levels, and obtain clarity. Billionaires are better able to manage the stresses of their hectic lifestyles by implementing these habits into their everyday routines.

Techniques for reducing stress

Although stress will always be a part of life, billionaires have found useful ways to reduce and manage its effects. By putting these techniques into practice, you can lower your stress levels and improve your general wellbeing.

Time for Introspection and Rest

Billionaires know how important it is to take some personal time to unwind and think. They find time in their hectic schedules to meditate, spend time in nature, or indulge in a hobby that helps them relax and refresh. Billionaires are able to gain perspective, lower stress levels, and preserve a sense of balance in their lives by making time for rest and introspection.

Outsourcing and delegation

Delegating and outsourcing work is a major stress management tactic used by billionaires. They realize they can't accomplish everything themselves and that they may devote more of their time and mental energy to more pressing issues by delegating some tasks to others. Billionaires are able to concentrate on their core competencies and goals by assigning responsibilities to competent individuals and outsourcing unnecessary chores.

Defining Limits

Billionaires understand that in order to safeguard their time and energy, boundaries must be created. They know that in order to keep their focus and avoid burnout, they must say "no" to some requests and commitments. Billionaires are able to safeguard their well-being and guarantee that they have the capacity to take on the most significant jobs and initiatives by establishing clear limits and placing their own needs first.

Looking for assistance

Even billionaires realize that they are not able to overcome obstacles in life on their own. They actively look for assistance from dependable mentors, coaches, and advisers who can offer direction, accountability, and a different viewpoint. Billionaires who have a robust support system around them are able to share their struggles, pick up insightful knowledge, and get the push they need to get over challenges.

Including self-care in your daily activities
After discussing the significance of stress management and self-care, it's time to think about how you may apply these concepts to your own life. The following are some doable actions you can take:

Establish a self-care schedule.
Create a self-care regimen that consists of things that feed your body, mind, and spirit. This could be doing physical activity, practicing meditation, reading, hanging out with loved ones, or picking up enjoyable hobbies. Make time for self-care a must in your weekly or daily routine.

Put mindfulness into practice.
By being completely present in the moment, you may incorporate mindfulness into your everyday life. Be mindful of your feelings, ideas, and bodily experiences without passing judgment. You can develop a stronger sense of wellbeing, improve focus, and lessen stress by engaging in this exercise.

Make recuperation and rest a priority.
Understand how crucial rest and recuperation are to preserving your general health. Make sure you get adequate sleep every night and give yourself regular breaks to rejuvenate during the day. Recall that getting enough sleep is essential for performing at your best and is not a sign of weakness.

Look for assistance.
Never hesitate to ask for help when you need it. Embrace a support system of dependable people who can offer direction, inspiration, and responsibility. Think about collaborating with a mentor or coach who can guide you through obstacles and help you reach your objectives.

Establish Limits
Establishing boundaries and saying "no" to obligations that conflict with your priorities or values are important life skills.

Put your attention where it counts and save time and energy. Keep in mind that you are saying "yes" to your own success and well-being when you say "no" to some things.

To sum up, billionaires and anyone else aiming to succeed and find fulfillment must practice self-care and stress management. Making time for your physical, mental, and emotional health is important because it will improve your performance, lower your stress level, and provide the groundwork for long-term success. When you apply these routines to your everyday life, you'll see a transformation in not only your own personal health but also your capacity to reach your objectives and positively influence the world.

FOSTERING INNOVATIVE THINKING

4.1 Welcome Originality and Inquisitiveness

Two characteristics that really set billionaires apart from the rest are creativity and curiosity. These prosperous people are aware of the value of thinking creatively, looking for fresh viewpoints, and taking measured risks. In this chapter, we will look at how engaging your curiosity and creativity may help you reach your greatest potential and achieve remarkable success.

4.1.1 The Creative Process's Power

The capacity to produce original concepts, ideas, and solutions is known as creativity. It is what propels advancement and innovation. Billionaires know that they need to constantly think outside the box and challenge the status quo in order to stay ahead in a world that is changing quickly. They actively look for chances to think creatively and accept it as an attitude.

You must liberate yourself from traditional thought patterns in order to develop your own creativity. Start by casting doubt on presumptions and opposing accepted conventions. Give yourself permission to experiment with unusual concepts and methods. Accept failure and embrace exploration; the most important lessons are often learned from mistakes.

4.1.2 Fostering Inquisitiveness

The drive to discover, investigate, and comprehend the world around us is known as curiosity. It is an essential quality that promotes creativity and individual development. Billionaires are driven to continuously seek out new experiences and information due to their unquenchable curiosity.

First and foremost, you must become insatiably curious. Read widely, experiment with various topics, and pursue lifelong learning. Make inquiries and look for responses. Have an open mind and be willing to consider fresh viewpoints. Accept the unknown and see obstacles as chances to improve.

4.1.3 Thinking Beyond the Box

Billionaires are renowned for their capacity for original thought. They take an unusual approach to issues and come up with creative fixes. Their distinctive capacity to think imaginatively and defy conventional thought patterns is what makes them unique.

In order to think creatively, you must confront your own prejudices and preconceptions. Venture beyond your comfort zone and investigate novel concepts and viewpoints. Assemble a varied group of people who can provide a range of perspectives and ideas. Welcome to brainstorming sessions and support unconventional ideas without passing judgment. You can seize new chances and possibilities by broadening your perspective and adopting unusual strategies.

4.1.4 Looking for Fresh Views

Billionaires know how important it is to look for fresh viewpoints. They actively seek out opposing ideas and associate with others who think differently than they do. They obtain a more comprehensive perspective of the world and become more capable of making well-informed decisions as a result.

Talk to individuals from other cultures and backgrounds in order to discover fresh viewpoints. Attend seminars and conferences to hear from professionals in a range of industries. Examine publications that present opposing views and make you reevaluate your own assumptions. Exposing oneself to a variety of viewpoints will help you think more broadly and acquire insightful knowledge that can propel your creativity and achievement.

4.1.5 Taking Reasonable Chances

Risk-taking is not a fear for billionaires. They realize that development and achievement require measured risks. They do not, however, take chances carelessly. Rather, they deliberate about the possible benefits and drawbacks before deciding.

It's critical to acquire as much information as you can before taking any calculated risks. Make sure you do your homework well, consider all of the possible outcomes, and balance the benefits and hazards. Create a risk management plan and ensure you have backup options. You can seize opportunities that others might pass up and catapult yourself into success by taking smart risks.

In conclusion, the key to attaining amazing success is to embrace innovation and curiosity. You can realize your full potential and reach greatness by thinking creatively, exploring fresh angles, and taking measured risks. Develop these behaviors in your own life, and you'll see unprecedented advancements in both your career and personal development.

4.2 Thinking Beyond the Box

Thinking creatively has become essential for success in the quickly evolving world of today. Billionaires are aware that the main forces behind growth and prosperity are creativity and invention. To solve issues and take advantage of opportunities, they consistently question received wisdom and look for fresh viewpoints. This section will look at the attitude and methods used by billionaires to think creatively and beyond the box to achieve their goals.

4.2.1 Welcome Originality and Inquisitiveness

Billionaires know that innovation is propelled by creativity. They actively seek out fresh concepts and opportunities, embracing their creative impulses. They know that creativity is based on curiosity, and they ask questions all the time to find fresh viewpoints and insights. Billionaires are able to see past the obvious and find original answers to challenging issues by fostering their curiosity.

In order to develop creativity and curiosity inside yourself, it's critical to establish an atmosphere that encourages experimenting and discovery. Take part in imaginative activities and surround yourself with a variety of viewpoints. Spend time reading widely, taking up new activities, and exposing oneself to a variety of experiences and civilizations. You can introduce yourself to fresh concepts and modes of thought by broadening your horizons.

4.2.2 Thinking Outside the Box

Billionaires are not limited by conventional lines or restrictions. They are adept at questioning accepted wisdom and thinking outside the box. They are aware that pushing the envelope of what is thought to be feasible frequently results in breakthroughs. Billionaires are able to see new markets, upend entire sectors, and develop ground-breaking solutions by thinking beyond the box.

Challenge the status quo and raise doubts about presumptions in order to cultivate an innovative attitude. Don't be scared to investigate novel concepts or question deeply established views. Be in the company of people who value and support your unconventional ideas. You can open up new possibilities and accomplish remarkable things by adopting an attitude of possibility and pushing the boundaries of what is thought to be normal.

4.2.3 Looking for Fresh Views

Billionaires recognize the importance of different points of view. They actively seek out opposing perspectives and associate with like-minded individuals. Billionaires are able to question their own presumptions and obtain fresh ideas by exposing themselves to a range of viewpoints. They are aware that by adopting a diverse perspective, they can find untapped potential and arrive at better conclusions.

In order to discover fresh viewpoints for yourself, it's

critical to interact with individuals from various cultures and backgrounds. Join networking groups, go to conferences, and take part in industry events to meet people with diverse perspectives. Make an effort to get input and pay attention to different viewpoints. You may broaden your thinking and arrive at better judgments by accepting variety and actively seeking out fresh viewpoints.

4.2.4 Taking Reasonable Chances

Taking calculated risks is frequently a necessary part of thinking beyond the box. Billionaires know that great achievement is rarely the result of playing it safe. In order to achieve their objectives, they are prepared to venture outside of their comfort zones and take measured risks. They see failure as a chance to develop and learn, and they recognize it as a normal part of the process.

It's critical to weigh the benefits and drawbacks of your decisions in order to cultivate a mindset that welcomes measured risks. Make sure you collect data, do in-depth research, and consult experts. You may make wise decisions and take calculated risks that could result in sizable returns by balancing the benefits and hazards.

In conclusion, billionaires have mastered the mentality of looking beyond the box. They are able to accomplish great achievement by embracing innovation and curiosity, thinking outside the box, seeking out fresh viewpoints, and taking measured risks. By implementing these routines and tactics in your own life, you can realize your greatest potential and forge an incredibly individual route to success. Dare to think creatively, question the status quo, and recognize the value of thinking beyond the box.

4.3 Looking for Fresh Views

Seeking out fresh viewpoints is a critical habit that separates billionaires from the rest in the fast-paced, constantly evolving world of business and entrepreneurship. These extremely successful people recognize the importance of novel concepts, contrasting opinions, and nontraditional ways of thinking. They understand that by accepting many viewpoints, they can find novel solutions, spot unexplored possibilities, and stay one step ahead of the competition.

4.3.1 Accepting Differences

To embrace diversity is one of the most important parts of looking for new insights. Billionaires are aware that interacting with people from other origins, cultures, and experiences can open their minds to a multitude of new perspectives. They actively look for those who can push their boundaries and offer fresh viewpoints.

Billionaires expose themselves to a wide range of perspectives and methods by cultivating a varied network. Their ability to think differently enables them to approach challenges from several perspectives and come up with original solutions that others might miss. They realize that diversity encourages inclusivity and an innovative culture within their firms, in addition to improving their decision-making process.

4.3.2 Leaving Your Comfort Zones Behind

Venturing beyond one's comfort zone is frequently necessary in search of fresh viewpoints. Billionaires don't hesitate to take risks and explore concepts that can seem outlandish or unorthodox. They are aware that pushing limits and questioning the status quo frequently leads to progress and breakthroughs.

Billionaires expose themselves to new experiences, cultures, and ways of thinking by venturing outside of their comfort zones. They actively look for chances to pick up knowledge from many fields, professions, and even pastimes. They gain a competitive edge from this idea exchange since it enables them to contribute novel perspectives and methods to their respective domains.

4.3.3 Taking Part in Active Hearing

Active listening is another crucial component in looking for fresh viewpoints. Billionaires know that hearing someone else's point of view isn't enough to fully comprehend their perspective. They actively listen in an effort to understand the underlying motives, principles, and convictions that influence those viewpoints.

Billionaires that actively listen to their clients, staff, and stakeholders are better able to comprehend their requirements, wants, and concerns. They may better satisfy the needs of their target audience by customizing their products, services, and tactics, thanks to this empathic approach. Additionally, it aids in strengthening their bonds with stakeholders and cultivates a spirit of loyalty and trust.

4.3.4 Accepting Change and Disruption

To seek fresh insights, one must also be open to change and upheaval. Billionaires are aware that things change quickly in this world, so what was effective one day could not be effective the next. To stay ahead of the curve, they actively search for disruptive technology, new trends, and altering market dynamics.

Billionaires adopt a disruptive and innovative approach to establish themselves as leaders in their industries. They don't hesitate to question accepted wisdom or investigate novel concepts. Their ability to adjust and progress enables them to grasp novel prospects, modify their approaches when needed, and preserve a competitive edge within a constantly evolving commercial environment.

4.3.5 Fostering an Attitude of Learning

Lastly, developing a learning mentality is necessary while looking for fresh viewpoints. Billionaires are aware that information is power and that ongoing education is crucial to both professional and personal development. They read a great deal and are always looking for fresh knowledge, concepts, and insights from a range of sources.

Billionaires increase their knowledge and expose themselves to new ideas by devoting time and energy to their education. To be at the forefront of their fields, they take part in workshops, attend conferences, and pursue continuing education. Their dedication to learning not only supports their individual development but also gives them the knowledge and confidence to confidently manage their businesses.

In conclusion, billionaires deliberately develop the practice of seeking out fresh viewpoints in order to fuel their success. Billionaires are able to find new opportunities, make smarter judgments, and remain ahead of the curve by embracing disruption and change, moving outside of their comfort zones, actively listening, and adopting a learning attitude. Readers can realize their full potential and experience amazing success in their own lives by forming this habit.

4.4 To achieve remarkable achievement, one must be willing to take chances. Billionaires know that in order to succeed, they have to be prepared to embrace uncertainty and venture outside of their comfort zones. It's crucial to remember, though, that billionaires do not take uninformed risks. They adopt a methodical and strategic approach, thoroughly weighing the advantages and disadvantages of each option before deciding. We will look at the attitude and tactics used by billionaires to take measured risks in this part.

4.4.1 Determining the Risk and Benefit

Billionaires carefully weigh the possible risks and rewards of any endeavor before committing to it or making a big choice. They are aware that there is uncertainty associated with all risks and that it is important to consider the possible outcomes. Billionaires are able to make well-informed judgments based on a comprehensive understanding of the prospective risks and rewards by carrying out extensive research and analysis.

Billionaires weigh a variety of considerations, including market trends, competition, financial ramifications, and possible returns, when determining how best to balance risk and reward. To acquire a thorough grasp of the circumstances, they perform feasibility studies, confer with specialists, and collect as much information as they can. This enables individuals to make well-considered choices that minimize possible losses while increasing their chances of success.

4.4.2 Overcoming Uncertainty and Fear

When one takes a risk, one naturally feels fear and uncertainty. But billionaires know how to go past these feelings and channel them into progress. They are aware that anxiety and dread frequently portend favorable circumstances for development and achievement. Billionaires embrace fear and utilize it as fuel to push themselves further, rather than letting it paralyze them.

Various tactics are used by billionaires to overcome anxiety and uncertainty. In order to lower uncertainty and boost their confidence when making decisions, they concentrate on acquiring knowledge and information. They also encircle themselves with a robust network of mentors and advisors who may offer direction and comfort in trying times. Billionaires are able to get over fear and take calculated risks because they have changed the way they think about dangers and see them as chances to thrive.

4.4.3 Making Knowledgeable Choices

Even in the face of uncertainty, billionaires are renowned for their capacity for well-informed decision-making. They realize that one of the most important abilities that can have a big impact on their achievement is decision-making. Billionaires analyze all the facts at their disposal and consult with several advisors before making a dangerous decision.

Billionaires use both analysis and intuition to make well-informed decisions. They follow their intuition, but they also validate it with facts and analysis. They speak with specialists, obtain information from a variety of sources, and ask reliable advisors for guidance. Billionaires are able to make well-rounded decisions that improve their chances of success by taking into account various points of view and performing in-depth studies.

4.4.4 Acquiring Knowledge from Setbacks

Taking chances will inevitably result in failure. Nonetheless, failure is not seen as a setback by billionaires but rather as an invaluable teaching opportunity. They are aware that failure can teach us important lessons and give us vital insights for our future endeavors. Rather than moping around their mistakes, billionaires figure out what went wrong, pinpoint areas where they can improve, and then modify their approach.

Billionaires are able to improve their strategy and raise their chances of success in subsequent undertakings by accepting failure and learning from it. They realize that failure is a necessary step on the path to development and improvement, rather than a reflection of their shortcomings. They are able to quickly recover from setbacks and carry on taking measured risks because of this approach.

To sum up, one of the most important things in attaining amazing success is to take calculated risks. Billionaires know how important it is to weigh the pros and cons, get over fear and uncertainty, make wise decisions, and learn from mistakes. Readers can get the strength and self-assurance needed to take calculated chances and elevate their own lives by implementing these tactics and mentalities.

BUILDING STRONG RELATIONSHIPS

5.1 Establishing Networks and Partnerships

Developing relationships and networking are crucial abilities for success in every industry. Billionaires actively build a strong network of contacts because they recognize the value of relationships. This section will discuss the value of networking, techniques for creating connections, and how to use these connections to further your objectives.

Networking's Power
There's more to networking than just trading business cards and going to parties. It's about establishing sincere connections with people who share your values so they can encourage and support you while you pursue achievement. Billionaires devote time and energy to cultivating their network because they understand that it is one of their most important assets.

Numerous advantages come from networking, such as cooperation, knowledge sharing, and access to new opportunities. Making connections with individuals from different industries and backgrounds can help you broaden your eyes, see the world from new angles, and benefit from their experiences. Furthermore, networking can lead to new business endeavors, collaborations, and mentorship opportunities.

Techniques for Establishing Relationships
Being proactive and showing real interest in other people are necessary for developing a solid network. The following techniques will assist you in creating deep connections:

1. Go to events for networking.
A fantastic way to meet people who share your interests is to attend industry conferences, seminars, and networking events. Professionals can network, share ideas, and consider possible collaborations at these events. To make a lasting impression, be ready with a succinct introduction and participate in thought-provoking discussions.

2. Make use of social media.
Social media platforms are an effective tool for networking in the modern digital age. Professionals may connect and interact

with others in their sector on LinkedIn in particular. Engage in active participation in pertinent organizations, distribute insightful content, and make contact with people who share your objectives and passions.

3. Look for guidance.
A beneficial relationship that can offer direction, encouragement, and insightful information is mentoring. Look for people who have succeeded in the area you want to work in, and make a sincere request for guidance. Show them that you value their time and are dedicated to your own development.

4. Become a member of trade associations.
Professional groups and organizations with a focus on a particular industry offer a venue for networking and keeping abreast of current advancements and trends. To gain a reputation and make contacts, get involved in these communities, go to events, and share your knowledge.

5. Provide value.
The process of networking is two-way. Give value to others without expecting anything in return in order to establish meaningful friendships. Assist others, impart your knowledge, and make connections amongst those who might find mutual benefit. Being a useful resource will attract people who value your contributions and share your interests.

Using relationships to your advantage
Creating a network is only the first step; it's also crucial to make use of such connections. The following tactics will assist you in maximizing the potential of your network:

1. Continue to communicate frequently.
It's important to be consistent when networking. Continue to stay in contact with your contacts by exchanging emails from time to time, getting together for coffee, or going to industry events together. Making regular contact keeps you in the forefront of people's minds when possibilities present themselves and helps to fortify relationships.

2. Work together and pool resources.

Seek out chances to work together with the people in your network. You may take on bigger initiatives, reach a wider audience, and succeed together by pooling your resources and talents. Be kind when it comes to providing your relationships with opportunities, introductions, and important resources. This mutual respect will fortify your bonds with one another and promote a supportive environment.

3. Request guidance and input.

Your network can offer insightful commentary and constructive criticism on your concepts and endeavors. Never be afraid to ask reliable contacts for suggestions or counsel. Their viewpoints can assist you in improving your tactics, spotting blind spots, and avoiding costly errors.

4. Give it away.

When you succeed, never forget to mentor and assist others as a way of giving back. Assist others in need of assistance, impart your knowledge and experiences, and establish connections between like-minded people. You make a good impact on the world and aid in the expansion and prosperity of your network by developing the talent of the future.

In summary

One of the most important habits of billionaires is networking and making relationships. You may quicken your own path to success by actively fostering relationships, looking for chances to connect, and using those connections for mutual gain. Recall that networking encompasses both your contributions and your opportunities for benefit. You build a network based on trust, cooperation, and mutual success by providing value and helping others.

5.2 Proficiency in Communication

One essential talent that is essential to the achievement of billionaires and anyone aiming for greatness is effective communication. It is essential for establishing trusting bonds, encouraging teamwork, and persuading people. This part aims to examine the fundamental elements of proficient communication and offer doable tactics to improve your communication abilities.

5.2.1 Paying attention

Active listening is one of the key components of good communication. Billionaires know how important it is to listen to and comprehend people fully. They are aware that listening intently enables them to learn important information, develop new perspectives, and forge closer bonds with others.

Your first step in becoming an engaged listener is to focus entirely on the speaker. Keep your eyes off other things and concentrate on their words, tone of voice, and body language. To demonstrate sincere interest, nod, keep eye contact, and use hints like "I see" or "Go on." Ask further inquiries to be sure you comprehend what they're saying.

5.2.2 Simple and Direct Communication

Billionaires are great at expressing themselves succinctly and plainly. They know that clarity and simplicity are necessary for effective communication. When speaking, make an effort to convey your views simply and without needless jargon or complications.

Before speaking or writing, arrange your ideas to improve clarity. Stick to your main arguments and speak in an easy-to-understand manner. Refrain from digressing or droning on.

Remember that succinct explanations frequently have a greater impact than long ones.

5.2.3 Nonverbal Correspondence
Nonverbal cues, like body language and facial expressions, are important tools for communicating ideas. Billionaires make use of non-verbal clues because they understand their power.

Keep an eye on your body language when speaking. Keep your stance open, create adequate eye contact, and highlight important points with movements. Genuine smiles help to create a happy and inviting environment. You can improve the efficacy of your communication and establish trust with people by coordinating your non-verbal clues with your spoken words.

5.2.4 Emotional Intelligence and Empathy
Billionaires understand the need for emotional intelligence and empathy in successful communication. They know that developing solid connections and settling disputes depend on one's ability to empathize with and understand others.

Put yourself in the other person's shoes and make an effort to comprehend their point of view in order to cultivate empathy. Be genuinely interested in learning about their experiences and sentiments. By acknowledging their experiences and reflecting back on their feelings, you can engage in active empathy. You may foster a secure and encouraging atmosphere for direct and honest conversation by exhibiting empathy.

5.2.5 Flexibility and adaptability
Adaptability and flexibility are critical communication abilities in a world that is changing quickly. Billionaires know how important it is to modify their communication style to fit various contexts and people.

Recognize other people's communication preferences to help you become more flexible. While some people might respond better to a more polite approach, others might prefer direct and assertive communication. You can build rapport and promote productive communication by modifying your communication style to suit the demands of others.

5.2.6 Handling of Conflicts

There will always be conflict in a partnership or group environment. Billionaires are excellent at communicating their way out of a situation. They know that keeping positive connections and accomplishing group objectives depend on timely and constructive dispute resolution.

Approach a conflict with an open mind and a cool demeanor. Encourage everyone engaged to voice their opinions by listening to them. Look for areas of agreement and concentrate on coming up with win-win solutions. Respect other people's ideas while expressing your demands and concerns through aggressive communication strategies. You may promote understanding and find solutions that work for everyone when you approach disagreements with empathy and an open mind.

5.2.7 Comments and Helpful Criticism

Billionaires see chances for development and progress in constructive criticism and feedback. They proactively solicit input from others and deliver it in a constructive and encouraging way.

Give constructive criticism of particular acts or behaviors rather than making personal jabs. Be precise, impartial, and offer doable recommendations for enhancement. When you're getting criticism, pay close attention and try not to get defensive. Consider criticism as a chance to improve and learn instead.

5.2.8 Ongoing Education and Development

One's ability to communicate effectively is a skill that is continually improving. Billionaires regularly look for opportunities to improve their communication skills because they recognize the value of lifelong learning.

Ask dependable mentors or coworkers for comments on your

communication so that you can keep getting better at it. Attend workshops or classes on communication techniques. Peruse literature or tune up to podcasts regarding efficient communication methods. Develop your abilities in a variety of contexts and consider your experiences to pinpoint areas that need work.

You may become a master communicator and improve your capacity to connect with people, form enduring bonds with others, and accomplish remarkable success by making a commitment to lifelong learning and development.

Recall that good communication involves more than just talking; it also entails building genuine connections with people, being aware of their needs, and delivering your message in a way that they can relate to. You may take advantage of new chances, motivate others, and move closer to becoming a billionaire by improving your communication abilities.

5.3 Cooperation and Group Dynamics
Working as a team and collaborating are crucial for success in any effort. Billionaires are aware of the benefits of collaborating with others to reach shared objectives and realize individual potential. We will discuss the value of cooperation and teamwork in the context of both professional and personal development in this part.

5.3.1 Harnessing the Strength of Teamwork
The act of cooperating with others to accomplish a shared

objective is known as collaboration. Billionaires understand that teamwork produces creative ideas, boosts productivity, and enhances problem-solving abilities. They know that they can accomplish significantly more as a team when they take advantage of the varied abilities, viewpoints, and experiences than they could alone.

Using a group's collective intellect is one of the main advantages of teamwork. When people collaborate and pool their knowledge and experience, they can provide fresh concepts and answers that could not have been thought of otherwise. Billionaires are capable of taking on difficult problems and coming up with innovative solutions because they combine their resources and work well together.

Team members' sense of camaraderie and support for one another is also fostered by collaboration. People that collaborate to achieve a common objective grow to have a feeling of purpose and a dedication to one other's success. Everyone feels appreciated and inspired to give their all in a good and encouraging work atmosphere as a result.

5.3.2 Establishing Productive Teams
For billionaires, creating cohesive teams is a critical competency. They know that putting together the ideal team of people with complimentary abilities and qualities is crucial to success. Billionaires carefully evaluate each member's special qualities and abilities as well as how they may contribute to the overall goals while building a team.

Billionaires place a high value on diversity and inclusiveness while forming a team. They understand that diverse teams generate more creative and comprehensive solutions because they bring a range of viewpoints and ideas to the table. Billionaires foster an environment where everyone feels appreciated and encouraged to share their special perspectives by embracing variety.

Billionaires also know how critical it is for team members to communicate clearly with one another. They create channels of communication that are open, support attentive listening, and advance transparency. Billionaires make sure that everyone on their team is informed, on the same page, and capable of working together efficiently by encouraging an environment of open and honest communication.

Within their teams, billionaires place a high value on mutual respect and trust in addition to communication. They foster an atmosphere where team members are comfortable taking chances, expressing their opinions, and making errors. Billionaires promote cooperation and teamwork by cultivating an environment of trust and respect, which helps their teams succeed.

5.3.3 Successful Teamwork Techniques

Billionaires use a range of tactics to encourage productive teamwork among its members. The following techniques can improve both individual and group collaboration:

Clearly outline the team's objectives and goals, and make sure that everyone on the team is aware of their respective roles and duties. This clarity avoids misunderstandings or effort duplication while assisting in bringing everyone together around a single goal.

Encourage honest and open communication: Encourage honest and open communication among team members. Establish a secure environment where team members can freely express their thoughts, worries, and criticism. Improved results are the result of this open communication, which also builds trust and collaborates.

Promote a variety of viewpoints: Welcome differences among team members and make an effort to find and consider their opinions. Team members should be encouraged to question presumptions, exercise critical thought, and offer their own perspectives. This variety of perspectives produces more creative and comprehensive answers.

Organize productive meetings: Make sure that team meetings are organized, targeted, and successful. Establish ground rules for involvement, set clear agendas, and motivate everyone on the team to actively participate. Having productive meetings keeps everyone informed, on the same page, and inspired.

Encourage team members to always learn new things and advance their careers by fostering a culture of continuous learning. Give people the chance to advance professionally, receive mentoring, and receive training. Billionaires foster an environment that values innovation and constant progress by investing in the team members' personal growth.

5.3.4 The Benefits of Teamwork for Personal Development

Working together is crucial for personal development as well as for success in the workplace. Working together, people can learn new things, see the world from different angles, and acquire useful talents.

People can learn from one another and expand their perspectives when they work together with people who possess varying abilities and areas of expertise. This exposure to many viewpoints and methods can encourage personal development, challenge preconceived notions, and inspire innovation.

Working together also gives people the chance to hone crucial interpersonal abilities like empathy, communication, and dispute resolution. People learn how to deal with diverse personalities, settle disputes, and forge enduring bonds through working with others. These abilities are helpful in everyday interactions and personal connections in addition to work environments.

In summary, cooperation and teamwork are critical behaviors

for success. Billionaires regularly look for chances to collaborate with others because they recognize the value of teamwork. Billionaires acquire remarkable outcomes by utilizing the varied abilities and viewpoints of a team. Collaboration improves problem-solving, stimulates creativity, and advances personal development in both work and personal contexts. People can succeed on a whole new level and improve their own lives by embracing teamwork and collaboration.

5.4 Establishing Credibility and Power

A key component of success in both personal and professional relationships is establishing influence and trust. Billionaires know how important it is to build solid relationships and earn people's trust. In this part, we will look at the techniques and mentalities that you may use to develop influence and trust in your own life.

5.4.1 Sincerity and Honesty

Authenticity is one of the keystones to establishing influence and trust. Billionaires know the value of staying loyal to who they are and what they believe in. They understand that people are more inclined to follow and trust those who are sincere and open.

Being a person of integrity is crucial for gaining power and trust. This entails acting in accordance with your statements and constantly exhibiting integrity, dependability, and honesty. When you behave in a trustworthy way on a regular basis, people will come to you more naturally, be open to your ideas, and be more inclined to follow your example.

5.4.2 Skillful Interaction

Another essential component in establishing influence and trust is effective communication. Billionaires are exceptional communicators who can express their ideas and opinions in a compelling and unambiguous manner. They are aware of how crucial it is to listen intently and show empathy in order to build deep relationships.

Engage in complete conversation with others and make an effort to grasp their points of view as you practice active listening to improve your communication skills. Ask intelligent questions and demonstrate a sincere interest in what they have to say. Work on enhancing your nonverbal and vocal communication abilities as well. Some examples of these include speaking with conviction and clarity, maintaining eye contact, and displaying confident body language.

5.4.3 Establishing Empathy and Rapport

Establishing rapport and empathy are critical to gaining influence and trust. Billionaires know how important it is to get to know people better and comprehend their wants and motives. Gaining empathy can help you relate to people more effectively and establish stronger bonds with them.

Practice putting yourself in other people's shoes and making an effort to comprehend their feelings and experiences in order to develop empathy and connection. Be genuinely empathetic by confirming their emotions. Find areas of agreement and shared interests as well to build rapport and a sense of connection.

5.4.4 Fulfilling Promises

Maintaining credibility and influence requires you to fulfill your commitments on a regular basis. Billionaires know how important it is to keep your word and perform to the highest standard. When you fulfill your commitments on a regular basis, you'll gain credibility with others.

Be honest about your capabilities and refrain from taking on more than you can handle in order to guarantee that you fulfill your commitments. Set priorities for your work and use your time wisely to make sure you can finish what you have to do. In the event that unanticipated events occur and you are unable to fulfill a commitment, be forthright and honest in your communication with the individuals concerned and endeavor to resolve the situation.

5.4.5 Establishing an Excellent Reputation

Billionaires are aware of the value of developing a stellar reputation. They aim for perfection in all they do because they understand that chances and doors can arise from having a solid reputation. You can establish a reputation that is respected and influential by continuously producing work of the highest caliber and going above and beyond expectations.

Establish high expectations for yourself and work tirelessly to surpass them if you want to gain a reputation for excellence. Always look for ways to grow and improve, and be prepared to go above and beyond to provide outstanding outcomes. Get input from others as well, and utilize it to improve your performance and hone your abilities.

5.4.6 Setting an Example

One of the most effective ways to gain influence and trust is to lead by example. Billionaires try to exhibit the traits and behaviors they would like to see in others because they know that deeds speak louder than words. You have the power to uplift and impact people around you by continuously exhibiting integrity, fortitude, and a strong work ethic.

To provide a good example, consider how your activities affect other people. Establish high expectations for yourself, and make sure you meet them. Have the courage to take on new tasks and show tenacity in the face of difficulties. One way to encourage others to follow your example is to set an example of the behaviors you want to see in them.

5.4.7 Establishing a Network of Reputable People

Building influence and trust requires surrounding oneself with people you can trust. Billionaires are aware of the benefits of a strong network and actively seek out connections with like-minded individuals. By establishing a network of reliable people, you may take advantage of their knowledge, assistance, and influence to further your own achievements.

In order to create a network of reliable people, concentrate on developing sincere relationships founded on respect and common ground. Look for chances to work together and encourage others to pursue their goals. Furthermore, take the initiative to cultivate and preserve your relationships by remaining in contact, lending support when required, and demonstrating a sincere interest in the accomplishments of others.

5.4.8 Accepting Authenticity and Vulnerability

Billionaires are aware that sincerity and vulnerability are effective strategies for gaining respect and power. They don't hesitate to discuss their failures and tribulations and to reveal their humanity. By embracing your genuineness and vulnerability, you can forge stronger bonds with people and win their trust and loyalty.

In order to embrace honesty and vulnerability, you must be open to sharing all of your experiences—both the good and the bad. Talk candidly about your struggles and the things you've discovered along the journey. By being vulnerable, you provide room for others to be vulnerable as well, which builds connection and trust.

Gaining influence and trust is a lifetime endeavor that calls for constant work and introspection. You can build solid connections, motivate others, and succeed more fully in all facets of your life by implementing the techniques and mental adjustments discussed in this section. Recall that developing influence and trust involves positively impacting others and actually engaging with them, not controlling or manipulating them.

DEVELOPING A
GROWTH MINDSET

6.1 Accepting Difficulties and Educational Possibilities

There will inevitably be obstacles and learning experiences on the path to success. One important habit of billionaires is to seize growth opportunities and embrace these challenges. They are aware that every challenge offers an opportunity to grow, learn, and eventually accomplish more success. This section will examine the mindset and techniques used by billionaires to welcome problems and transform them into worthwhile educational opportunities.

6.1.1 A Growth Mindset's Power

Developing a growth mentality is one of the core elements of accepting challenges. Billionaires know that brains and skills can be acquired with commitment and hard work. They think that failing is a chance to learn and improve, rather than a reflection on their value. They can tackle problems with resiliency and determination when they have a growth attitude.

In order to cultivate a growth mindset, it's critical to reinterpret failure. Consider failure a stepping stone toward progress rather than a setback. Acknowledge your errors, consider what went wrong, and apply what you've learned to move forward. Accept obstacles as chances to improve your skills and broaden your knowledge.

6.1.2 Acknowledging Unease

Billionaires know that pushing outside their comfort zones is necessary for growth and success. They deliberately seek out discomfort, viewing it as a motivator for both career and personal development. They can find new qualities and capacities by pushing themselves past their comfort zones.

The first step in embracing discomfort is to pinpoint the areas of your life where you feel uninspired or unfulfilled. These are the locations most in need of development. Gradually push yourself beyond your comfort zone by taking tiny actions. This could include acquiring a new skill, taking on challenging responsibilities at work, or participating in physically or psychologically taxing activities. Accepting discomfort will help you grow as a person and create new opportunities.

6.1.3 Taking Failures to Heart

Failure is a necessary component of any path to success. Billionaires know that failing is not fatal but rather a useful teaching tool. They see failure as an opportunity to improve, and they take it to heart. They are able to make wiser decisions and ultimately succeed more when they learn from their failures.

It's critical to have a growth mentality and face failure with an open mind in order to learn from it successfully. Consider the mistakes that were made, note the lessons that were discovered, and apply this understanding to future planning and development. Accept failure as a chance to learn important lessons and improve your strategy.

6.1.4 Requesting Mentorship and Input

Billionaires know how important it is to ask for advice and input from others. They actively look for mentors who, based on their own experiences, can offer insightful advice. Billionaires can quicken their learning and development by surrounding themselves with smart and accomplished people.

The first step in getting advice and mentoring is to find people who have succeeded in the fields in which you want to be an expert. Make contact with them and let them know how much you admire their accomplishments. Seek their advice and solicit their opinions on your own objectives and tactics. Accept constructive criticism with an open mind and seize the chance it presents to grow.

6.1.5 Adopting a Philosophy of Lifelong Learning

Billionaires know that education is an ongoing process. They are always looking to learn new things and keep up with advancements and trends in the business. Through constant learning, attending seminars, and reading books, they make an investment in their own personal development.

Make learning a priority in your life if you want to adopt

an attitude of continuous learning. Allocate specific time for reading, participating in workshops, or enrolling in online courses. Continue to be inquisitive and receptive, constantly searching for fresh insights. Gaining more information and learning new things all the time will make you more capable of overcoming obstacles and taking advantage of chances.

In summary
One essential habit of billionaires is to welcome opportunities for learning and challenges. You can develop this habit in your own life by adopting a growth attitude, accepting discomfort, learning from mistakes, asking for help and mentoring, and embracing a lifetime learning mindset. Recall that obstacles are actually opportunities for growth rather than impediments to achievement. Accept them, draw lessons from them, and utilize them to drive yourself to new heights.

6.2 Taking a Positive Viewpoint

Positivity is a strong asset that can have a big impact on both your personal and professional lives. It's a way of thinking that enables you to take on obstacles head-on, see the good in any circumstance, and remain resilient when faced with hardship. This section will discuss the value of having a positive outlook and how it can help you on your path to success.

The influence of hope
Being positive is a way of life, not just a mental condition. You become more open to a world of opportunities when you embrace positivity. You develop greater adaptability, resilience, and open-mindedness. When you are positive, you can view obstacles as chances for improvement and education rather than as failures. It gives you the ability to approach problems with a solution-focused mindset and come up with original solutions to problems.

Changing your viewpoint

Changing your viewpoint is the first step towards embracing a good outlook. Teach yourself to focus on the positive aspects of your life rather than what is lacking or wrong. This does not imply putting up with difficulties or acting as though everything is ideal. It entails accepting the challenges as well as the chances for development and advancement.

Developing Appreciation

Developing thankfulness is one of the best strategies for changing your mindset. Every day, set aside some time to think about your blessings. It could be anything as straightforward as a stunning sunset, a buddy who is encouraging, or a minor victory. You may educate your mind to perceive the good in every scenario by concentrating on the positive parts of your life.

Filling your environment with goodness

The individuals you spend a lot of time with greatly influence your attitude and way of thinking. Assemble a circle of upbeat, encouraging people who encourage and inspire you. Look for mentors and role models who share the values and way of thinking that you find inspiring. Talk to people who are upbeat and encouraging, and try to avoid being around negative people or things on social media, in the news, or in unhealthy relationships.

Using Positive Self-Talk Techniques

Your attitude and sense of self are greatly influenced by the words you use to speak to yourself. Use affirmations and empowering words to replace self-doubt and negative ideas while you engage in positive self-talk. Rephrase it to something like, "I am capable of overcoming any challenge," as opposed to, "I can't do this." You have the ability to reprogram your brain to focus on opportunities and solutions by intentionally using positive language.

Accepting Failure as a Chance to Learn

Having a positive outlook makes it possible to view failure as a teaching tool rather than a setback. Consider your mistakes as stepping stones to success rather than as something to linger on or as a source of defeat. Take what you've learned from your mistakes, modify your strategy, and keep going forward with optimism. Recall that all successful people have experienced setbacks. Your final success is determined by how you handle them.

Embracing the Journey with Joy

Having a positive outlook entails appreciating the trip as much as the outcome. No matter how tiny your progress may be, acknowledge it and value the experiences and lessons you gain along the way. Let go of the demand for instant gratification and enjoy the process of personal development. You may build a happy and meaningful life by choosing to be joyful in the here and now.

Getting Rid of Negativity Bias

Humans are predisposed to focus more on unpleasant memories and ideas. Our capacity to adopt an optimistic outlook may be hampered by this negative bias. Acknowledge this prejudice and make a conscious decision to pay attention to the good things in your life. Positive ideas should be used to counter negative ones. You can train your brain to automatically adopt a happy outlook over time.

Developing Resilience

Resilience and optimism are closely related. It enables you to overcome obstacles, adjust to change, and recover from setbacks. Develop coping strategies for stress, self-care, and a solid support network to help you become more resilient. By taking care of your mental and emotional health, you make it easier for yourself to remain upbeat even in trying circumstances.

Adopting a Growth Perspective

One of the main elements of a growth mentality is optimism. Accept the idea that, with commitment and effort, you can improve your skills and intelligence. Rather than viewing obstacles as dangers to your self-worth, view them as chances for personal development. You approach life with curiosity, resiliency, and self-belief when you have a growth mentality.

To sum up, cultivating an optimistic outlook is a life-changing behavior that can help you achieve success. It enables you to keep a resilient attitude, confront obstacles with optimism, and recognize opportunities in any circumstance. Through perspective-changing, practicing thankfulness, and surrounding yourself with good people, you can cultivate a positive mindset that will enable you to overcome challenges and realize your objectives. Accept the power of optimism and see how it changes every area of your life.

6.3 Keeping Going Despite Setbacks

One quality that really separates billionaires from the rest is persistence. They have an unflinching will to keep moving forward in the face of difficulties and setbacks. They are aware that obstacles must be overcome in order to reach greatness and that success does not come easily. This section will discuss the value of persevering in the face of setbacks and provide tips on how to develop this crucial trait in your own life.

6.3.1 Seeing Opportunities in Difficulties

Billionaires see obstacles as chances for development and education. They are aware that every challenge offers an opportunity to grow, learn from mistakes, and improve tactics. They meet obstacles head-on, not running from them, understanding that getting beyond obstacles is a necessary step on the path to success.

It's crucial to change the way you view obstacles in order

to develop this way of thinking. Consider them as stepping stones toward your objectives rather than obstacles. Accept the discomfort and uncertainty that come with overcoming challenges because you will need them to advance both personally and professionally.

6.3.2 Building Up Your Resilience

Being resilient means having the capacity to pick oneself up after failures and carry on. Billionaires know that failing is merely a necessary step on the path to success rather than the end. They cultivate a resilient mindset that enables them to overcome obstacles, adjust their approach, and learn from their mistakes.

Cultivating a growth mindset is essential to building resilience. Accept the idea that failure is a chance to grow rather than a reflection of your skills. Consider the lessons they have taught you and apply them to your future endeavors rather than obsessing over past failures.

Resilience can also be increased by engaging in self-care and stress-reduction activities. Give yourself some time to rest and recuperate, both mentally and physically. Take part in things that make you happy and contribute to your optimistic mindset. You will be more prepared to take on difficulties and persevere in the face of setbacks if you take care of yourself.

6.3.3 Having Reasonably High Standards

Billionaires know how important it is to have reasonable expectations. They are aware that obstacles are a normal part of the path and that success requires patience and hard work. When faced with challenges and disappointments, they don't give up since they have reasonable expectations.

It is essential to have a clear grasp of your goals and the steps necessary to attain them in order to create reasonable expectations. Make a schedule for completing the smaller, more doable chores that will help you achieve your goals. This will support you in maintaining your motivation and attention in the face of obstacles.

It's also critical to keep in mind that development is not necessarily linear. It's important to recognize and appreciate little triumphs along the journey since there will be ups and downs. When you recognize and value your accomplishments, you will maintain your drive and tenacity in the face of setbacks.

6.3.4 Looking for assistance and cooperation

Billionaires know the value of teamwork and asking for help when things get tough. They surround themselves with a network of like-minded people, mentors, and advisors who can offer support and direction when things get tough.

It's critical to have a robust support system in order to foster this behavior. Look for mentors who have been through comparable experiences and who can provide insightful commentary and guidance. Work together with people who can help and inspire you along the path and who have similar aims to yours.

Furthermore, never hesitate to seek assistance when necessary. Realize that asking for help is a strength rather than a sign of weakness. You can persevere in the face of difficulties and surmount hurdles more skillfully by making use of the knowledge and experience of others.

6.3.5 Taking Failures to Heart

Billionaires see failure as an important teaching tool. They are aware that failures and errors are a necessary part of the journey to achievement. Rather than moping around defeat, they dissect their errors, take away important lessons, and apply those lessons to their future strategy.

It's critical to approach failure with a growth mindset in order to develop this habit. Consider it an opportunity to grow and learn, rather than a reflection of your own skills. Give your failures some thought, determine the lessons they have taught you, and use those lessons in your next attempts.

It's also critical to adopt a mindset that values ongoing

education. Seek out fresh information and abilities that will enable you to conquer challenges with more efficiency. You can strengthen your ability to persevere in the face of difficulties by continuously learning new things and using what you've learned from both successes and mistakes.

In summary
One essential behavior for success is the ability to persevere in the face of setbacks. Although billionaires are aware that failures are unavoidable, what makes them unique is their steadfast resolve and fortitude. You can create the habit of persistence in your own life by accepting problems as opportunities, being resilient, establishing reasonable expectations, asking for help, and learning from your mistakes. Recall that while success does not come easily, you can overcome any challenge and accomplish amazing things if you are persistent and have a development mentality.

6.4 Ongoing Education and Development
A commitment to lifelong learning and development is a necessary habit for billionaires and other successful people. Since the world is always changing, those who are prepared to change and develop will have a distinct advantage. We will discuss the value of investing in personal development, the significance of lifelong learning, and methods for ongoing progress in this part.

6.4.1 Lifelong Learning's Power
Billionaires know that education is an ongoing process. They understand that information is power and that maintaining an open mind and curiosity are essential for both professional and personal development. People who pursue lifelong learning are better equipped to stay current, adjust to shifting conditions, and take advantage of new opportunities.

Billionaires place a high value on education and actively seek out new information in all media in order to embrace lifelong learning. They take online courses, read books, go to conferences and seminars, and have in-depth discussions with professionals in their domains. They are aware that learning occurs not only in formal education but also in casual encounters and conversations.

6.4.2 Reading and Getting Knowledge

A frequent habit among billionaires is their insatiable need for reading. They are aware that books contain a wealth of knowledge and understanding from some of history's brightest minds. Through reading, they can broaden their knowledge, see things from other angles, and be more creative.

Billionaires read every day and commit time to the activity. Whether it's self-help books, industry-specific literature, or biographies of famous people, they give priority to publications that fit their interests and aspirations. They keep on top of things and are better able to make decisions since they read and learn new things on a regular basis.

6.4.3 Looking for Mentors and Emulations

Billionaires understand the importance of taking advice from people who have already succeeded. They actively look for mentors and role models who are able to offer advice, share their experiences, and impart insightful knowledge. A mentor can help people overcome obstacles and steer clear of frequent mistakes by offering a road map for success.

Billionaires network and establish relationships with key players in their industry in order to locate mentors. They approach mentoring relationships with an open mind and a humble demeanor. Through utilizing the knowledge and experience of mentors, billionaires can quicken their learning and development and gain insightful knowledge that can help them succeed.

6.4.4 Putting Money Into Personal Development

Billionaires know that investing in their own personal development pays off in the long run. They put their own growth first, devoting time, energy, and resources to pursuits that improve their abilities, expertise, and outlook. They understand that they can succeed more in every aspect of life if they work on always bettering themselves.

There are various ways to invest in one's own development. It could entail joining mastermind groups, hiring coaches or consultants, or going to workshops and seminars. Introspection and self-reflection are also practices carried out by billionaires in an effort to identify their areas of strength, weakness, and growth. They become better leaders, decision-makers, and innovators when they invest in themselves.

6.4.5 Methods for Ongoing Enhancement
Billionaires use a variety of tactics to make sure that their lives are always getting better. They set clear goals and evaluate their progress on a regular basis. They use feedback as a tool for development, asking colleagues and trusted advisors for their opinions. They welcome challenges and see failures as chances for growth and development.

Billionaires also place a high value on their well-being and self-care in order to promote ongoing progress. They are aware that in order to continue performing at a high level, one must maintain both physical and mental health. To refuel and revitalize themselves, they partake in exercises, mindfulness, and meditation.

Billionaires also have a growth mentality, which is the conviction that one can improve one's intelligence and skills through commitment and hard work. They see mistakes as important teaching moments and accept failure as a necessary step on the path to achievement. They maintain their resilience in the face of challenges and disappointments by embracing a growth mentality and never stopping trying to get better.

In conclusion, the core values of billionaires are lifelong learning and personal development. People can reach amazing achievement and realize their full potential by adopting techniques for continual improvement, investing in personal growth, reading, seeking mentors, and embracing lifelong learning. Success is a never-ending journey, and those who make the commitment to never stop learning and growing will always be one step ahead of the competition.

TAKING CALCULATED RISKS

7.1 Evaluating the Risk and Benefit

One of the most important differences between regular people and billionaires is their ability to weigh risk and reward. Billionaires know how important it is to make wise judgments and take calculated risks in order to attain amazing success. They can make calculated decisions that can result in large profits because they have mastered the art of weighing possible risks and rewards. In this part, we will examine the attitude and techniques used by billionaires to weigh risk and return.

The Significance of Risk Evaluation
Billionaires are aware that success requires taking calculated risks. They do acknowledge the necessity of carefully weighing these dangers, though. They don't just seize opportunities without thinking through the possible repercussions. Rather, they adopt a methodical approach, carefully considering the advantages and disadvantages.

Billionaires weigh a variety of criteria, including market circumstances, competition, and potential roadblocks, when evaluating risk. To obtain a thorough grasp of the current situation, they carry out an in-depth investigation and study. They are then in a position to make well-informed choices that increase the possibility of success and reduce the possibility of failure.

Assessing possible benefits
Billionaires are skilled at not only identifying dangers but also estimating possible returns. They realize that putting their time and money at risk in the absence of substantial returns is not a prudent use of both. As a result, before acting, they thoroughly consider the possible benefits of any chance.

When assessing prospects, billionaires take both short- and long-term profits into account. They concentrate on the possibility of long-term profitability and expansion rather than short-term advantages. They make sure that their choices are in line with their long-term objectives and desires by doing this.

Creating a Mentality of Risk-Taking
Becoming fearless in the face of uncertainty is one of the

most important characteristics of billionaires. They've acquired a risk-taking mentality that enables them to seize chances even when they could end up failing. They are prepared to venture outside of their comfort zones in order to achieve their objectives because they recognize that taking chances is essential for growth.

Billionaires foster a growth-oriented mindset by adopting a positive outlook on failure. Instead of seeing failure as a setback, they see it as a teaching opportunity. They are aware that every setback yields priceless lessons and revelations that can be used in subsequent undertakings. Billionaires are able to take chances with confidence because they are able to reframe failure in this way: even if they fail, they will still have gained invaluable experience and knowledge.

Making knowledgeable choices
Billionaires are renowned for their capacity for reasoned decision-making. They don't make snap decisions or follow their instincts. Rather, they try to obtain as much information as they can and thoroughly consider it before deciding. To make sure they have a thorough grasp of the problem, they confer with specialists, carry out market research, and ask reliable consultants for guidance.

Billionaires take into account both qualitative and quantitative aspects while making judgments. To evaluate the possible risks and rewards, they examine financial data, industry projections, and market trends. In addition, they consider their own instincts and intuition, drawing guidance from their years of experience and knowledge.

Acquiring Knowledge from Setbacks
Billionaires try to make wise choices, but they also realize that mistakes can happen occasionally. They don't let failure deter them, though. Rather, they see it as a chance for development and education. They examine their mistakes, determine what went wrong, and apply what they've learned to make better

decisions going forward.

Billionaires are able to improve their ability to analyze risk by learning from their mistakes. They get better at seeing possible hazards and staying clear of them. They also develop greater resilience, rising above setbacks with redoubled resolve and a sharper sense of purpose.

Juggling Benefit and Risk

Evaluating risk and reward does not mean taking every risk or seizing every chance without thinking things through. It involves striking the ideal ratio between profit and risk. Billionaires know that, although avoiding risks entirely can result in missed opportunities for growth and success, taking excessive risks can cause catastrophic losses.

Billionaires use a combination of experience, intuition, and meticulous analysis to find the correct balance. They weigh the possible benefits against the possible hazards, and they decide based on their long-term objectives and risk tolerance. They take calculated chances without fear, but they also use care and prudence to safeguard their assets and interests.

In conclusion, one crucial ability that billionaires possess is the ability to weigh risk and return. They are able to make wise judgments that lead them to success by carefully weighing the benefits and hazards that could arise. They acquire a risk-taking mentality, accept failure as a teaching tool, and base their choices on in-depth investigation and analysis. Billionaires are able to build enduring wealth and achieve incredible achievements by finding the ideal balance between risk and reward.

7.2 Overcoming Uncertainty and Fear

Two strong emotions that can prevent us from realizing our full potential are fear and uncertainty. They have the power to immobilize us, keeping us from taking calculated chances and acting bravely when they are frequently needed to accomplish great accomplishments. This section will examine the methods and mentalities that billionaires use to get over fear and uncertainty, which enables them to venture into unknown areas and take advantage of chances that others might pass over.

7.2.1 Accepting Fear as a Growth-Catalyst

Humans naturally react with fear to the unknown. It is the body's defense mechanism against possible danger. Billionaires, nevertheless, are aware that fear may also spur development. They now know how to welcome their fear and turn it into a motivating factor to move forward. Rather than letting fear stop them, they use it as inspiration and drive to get things done.

Billionaires use a growth mindset in order to conquer fear. For them, obstacles and ambiguities present chances for growth and learning. They are prepared to venture into the unknown, even if it means confronting their fears, because they recognize that progress happens when they are uncomfortable. Billionaires overcome their obstacles and accomplish amazing achievements by reinterpreting fear as a sign of development and progress.

7.2.2 Developing Resilience Despite Uncertainty

Billionaires recognize that uncertainty is a natural element of life and that they cannot control every situation. Rather than permitting uncertainty to discourage people, they foster adaptation and resilience. They understand that failures and setbacks are unavoidable, but what makes them unique is their capacity to overcome these obstacles and grow from them.

Billionaires build a strong sense of confidence and self-belief in order to nurture resilience. They have confidence in their skills and resist being influenced by other factors. They see obstacles as chances for development and progress and are aware that setbacks are only temporary. Billionaires are able to face uncertainty head-on by redefining obstacles as opportunities for growth and achievement.

7.2.3 Looking for information and knowledge
Information and knowledge are two of the best strategies to combat fear and uncertainty. Billionaires look for information from a range of sources because they recognize how important it is to be well-informed. They keep abreast of developments in the market, upcoming technology, and industry trends. They can reduce risks and make educated judgments when they are well-informed.

Billionaires also encircle themselves with a network of mentors and specialists who can offer advice and assistance. They can provide insightful advice and recognize the importance of learning from others who have already faced comparable difficulties. Billionaires are able to make more thoughtful judgments and obtain a better knowledge of the risks by consulting with experts and considering many viewpoints.

7.2.4 Creating an Upbeat Attitude
Encouraging thoughts are essential when addressing anxiety and uncertainty. Billionaires deliberately choose to concentrate on optimism and positivity because they recognize that their thoughts and beliefs influence their reality. They develop an attitude of abundance and thankfulness, thinking that

possibilities are constantly present to them—even in the face of uncertainty.

Billionaires use regular visualization exercises and mantras to cultivate a good mindset. They declare their confidence in their capacity to overcome obstacles and envision the results they hope to achieve. Billionaires are able to reprogram their brains and cultivate a robust mindset that can survive fear and uncertainty by constantly reinforcing positive thoughts and beliefs.

7.2.5 Taking Reasonably High Risks

Billionaires know that success requires taking calculated risks, even in the face of fear and uncertainty. They carefully weigh the advantages and disadvantages of every opportunity, and they base their choices on in-depth research. Even though they are aware that not all chances will pay off, they are nonetheless willing to take a chance if the possible gain justifies the possible danger.

Billionaires learn to trust their gut feelings and have a keen sense of intuition in order to take measured risks. They recognize that sometimes they must follow their instincts in addition to using their knowledge and experience as a guide. Billionaires are able to make audacious decisions that result in amazing achievements by developing their decision-making abilities and having faith in their judgment.

In conclusion, pursuing achievement will inevitably involve dread and uncertainty. Billionaires, on the other hand, have perfected the technique of conquering these feelings and turning them into drivers of development. Through the acceptance of fear, building resilience, learning new things, adopting an optimistic outlook, and taking measured chances, they manage to venture into unfamiliar areas and grasp chances that others may avoid. Readers can likewise conquer fear and uncertainty and take their own lives to new heights of achievement by implementing these techniques and mentalities.

7.3 Making Knowledgeable Choices

Making well-informed decisions is a critical ability that separates billionaires from the general population. This chapter will examine the methods and frame of mind required to make wise decisions that can result in success. Readers will acquire the ability to make well-informed decisions that are consistent with their objectives and aspirations by comprehending the significance of obtaining information, evaluating risks, and taking prospective consequences into account.

7.3.1 Information's Power

Knowledge is the cornerstone on which well-informed judgments are constructed. Billionaires know how important it is to have precise and pertinent information before making any big decisions. They understand that judgments taken in the absence of sufficient knowledge can result in expensive errors and lost opportunities.

In order to make well-informed decisions, comprehensive research and data collection from reputable sources are important. This could entail researching market patterns, examining financial statements, or consulting with professionals in the field. Billionaires gain a deep awareness of the variables that can affect their actions by learning as much as possible.

7.3.2 Examining the Benefits and Risks

There is some risk involved in every action, and billionaires are adept at identifying and controlling it. They are aware that development and success depend on taking measured risks. They do understand the significance of balancing the possible benefits with the potential drawbacks, though.

Analyzing the risks and potential rewards is essential when making well-informed decisions. This calls for a thorough analysis of the possible outcomes and a comprehension of the likelihood of success. Billionaires can make decisions with a higher chance of success by carrying out a comprehensive risk analysis.

7.3.3 Taking into Account Different Viewpoints

Billionaires know how crucial it is to consider a variety of viewpoints before making big decisions. They understand that their personal prejudices and constrained perspectives can make it difficult for them to perceive the wider picture. They can develop a more thorough grasp of the situation and make better decisions by taking into account many points of view.

It is helpful to get advice from mentors, coworkers, or reliable advisors when making decisions. Through active listening to other perspectives and participating in productive dialogues, readers can acquire significant understandings that can influence their decision-making process. Making educated selections is more likely when this approach is used since it enables a more comprehensive evaluation of the circumstances.

7.3.4 Comparing the Short- and Long-Term Effects

When it comes to making decisions, billionaires think long-term. They are aware that their long-term objectives might not always coincide with short-term successes. They think about the long-term effects of their choices rather than just the short-term gains.

It's critical to consider any possible long-term effects while making decisions. This entails taking into account potential effects on relationships, opportunities in the future, and ultimate objectives. Billionaires are able to make decisions that are in line with their vision and promote sustainable growth by putting long-term success ahead of short-term satisfaction.

7.3.5 Believing Your Gut Sentiment and Intuition

Billionaires rely on their gut instincts and intuition in addition to data and analysis when making judgments. They are aware that their gut feelings are an effective instrument that can help them navigate unclear circumstances. Billionaires are able to make well-informed and instinct-driven decisions by fusing logical reasoning with intuitive understanding.

In order to access intuition, one must develop self-awareness and have faith in their inner guidance. This entails listening to one's feelings, observing small clues, and keeping an open mind to intuitive revelations. By developing this ability, readers will be able to make choices that are informed by both reason and a thorough comprehension of both the circumstances and themselves.

7.3.6 Pursuing Ongoing Education

Billionaires are dedicated to lifelong learning and have a voracious appetite for information. They are aware that things change all the time and that being informed is essential to making wise choices. Billionaires make sure they have the information and abilities needed to make wise decisions by making investments in their own personal development and progress.

Adopting a lifelong learning mindset is crucial for making informed judgments. This entails constantly broadening one's knowledge base, looking for fresh information, and remaining current with industry trends. Readers who make a commitment to lifelong learning can arm themselves with the knowledge and understanding required to make wise choices in a world that is constantly changing.

7.3.7 Taking Initiative and Assessing Outcomes

Billionaires know that taking action and assessing the outcome is just as important as making well-informed decisions. They understand that decisions are only worthwhile if they are followed by resolute action and an openness to absorb the lessons that come from the results.

It is essential to lean toward action in order to make well-informed decisions. This entails making decisions quickly and keeping a careful eye on the outcomes. Billionaires can improve their decision-making process, learn from their mistakes and triumphs, and make any required changes by assessing the results.

To sum up, the ability to make well-informed decisions is a crucial competency that can help people achieve success. Readers can make decisions that are in line with their objectives and aspirations by obtaining information, assessing risks, taking into account many viewpoints, and balancing short-term vs. long-term effects. They may negotiate the difficulties of decision-making and raise their odds of astounding achievement by following their gut, pursuing lifelong learning, and acting.

7.4 Taking Lessons from Mistakes

Failure is a necessary part of life, and millionaires are no exception. Actually, a lot of the most successful people in the world credit their successes to the lessons they took from their mistakes. This section will discuss the value of learning from mistakes and how they can spur achievement and personal development.

7.4.1 Seeing Failure as a Chance to Learn

Billionaires know that failing is merely a necessary step on the path to success rather than the end. They accept failure as a useful teaching tool and apply it to improve their methods and techniques. Setbacks don't depress them; instead, they see them as insightful criticism that helps them make better choices and take appropriate action.

Billionaires, when faced with failure, pause to consider what went wrong and why. In an effort to identify the underlying reasons for their weaknesses, they examine their errors and inadequacies. They learn a great deal about their own advantages and disadvantages by doing this, which helps them make better judgments in the future.

7.4.2 Drawing Inferences and Modifying Approaches
Learning from mistakes means taking important lessons to heart and modifying plans of action accordingly. Billionaires know that failing is a chance to learn and grow, rather than a reflection of their value or competence. They have a growth mentality and approach failure with the idea that they can improve and grow from their errors.

Billionaires evaluate their mistakes and modify their tactics and methods accordingly. They are prepared to change course and attempt different strategies because they recognize that what has worked in the past might not work in the future. They are able to overcome setbacks and attain sustained success because of their adaptability and readiness to change.

7.4.3 Fostering Perseverance and Resilience
While failure can be emotionally taxing, millionaires have cultivated a great degree of fortitude and resilience. They are aware that failures are fleeting and that it frequently takes several tries to succeed. When faced with failure, they don't give up; instead, they utilize it as motivation to keep going.

Billionaires have a mentality that views failure as an essential step on the path to success. They see every setback as a learning opportunity that advances them toward their objectives. They are able to overcome obstacles with this mentality and keep their will and focus.

7.4.4 Fostering a Growth-Based Perspective
A growth mindset, or the conviction that skills and intellect can be acquired through commitment and effort, is necessary for learning from failure. Billionaires are aware that, with enough work and education, they can develop their abilities rather

than having them fixed. They view failure as a chance to push themselves beyond their comfort zones.

Billionaires have a growth attitude that encourages them to take chances and venture outside of their comfort zones. They are aware that making mistakes is a necessary component of learning and that it is through making mistakes that they might find new paths and chances. With the knowledge that even in the event of failure, students will still have gained invaluable knowledge and experience, this mindset enables them to approach difficulties with curiosity and enthusiasm.

7.4.5 Creating Success Out of Failure

Not only should errors be examined and corrected, but failure can also be leveraged as a springboard for achievement. Billionaires are aware that failure can offer them special perspectives and insights that can give them a competitive advantage.

Billionaires are able to recognize fresh possibilities and strategies that others might have missed by taking lessons from their mistakes. They leverage their newfound knowledge and experience to produce ground-breaking solutions, using their failures as a platform for creativity and innovation.

In summary, failure is something to be welcomed and learned from, rather than something to be feared or avoided. Billionaires view failure as a potent instrument for personal development and recognize it as a necessary component of the path to success. Billionaires attain incredible levels of success by accepting failure as a teaching opportunity, drawing lessons from it, modifying their approaches, strengthening their resilience, adopting a growth mindset, and transforming failure into success. As readers, we can use these routines and mentalities to help us negotiate our own setbacks and turn them into opportunities for growth and achievement.

CREATING A WEALTH MINDSET

8.1 Changing Your Perspective on Money

In our lives, money is a great force. It can give us independence, security, and the chance to follow our goals. But when it comes to money, a lot of us have unfavorable connections and restricting views. These ideas may prevent us from reaching abundance and financial success. To genuinely generate riches and lead an abundant life, we must change our perspective on money.

8.1.1 Recognizing Your Present Financial Attitude

Prior to changing our financial thinking, it's critical to recognize the attitudes and beliefs we already have about money. Think for a moment about how you personally feel about money. What financial education did you receive as a child? When you consider money, how does it make you feel? Do you think there is an abundance or a scarcity of money? Do you find the concept of wealth to be comfortable?

Our financial perspective is frequently influenced by our cultural background, upbringing, and prior experiences. We may have grown up with unfavorable attitudes and anxieties around money if we were reared in a setting where it was perceived as scarce or wicked. These ideas may manifest in self-defeating actions like hoarding money, lying about our value, or passing up financial chances.

8.1.2 Questioning Limiting Thoughts

It's critical to question and modify our limiting assumptions about money after we've identified them. Many of our financial assumptions are the product of misinformation and societal indoctrination rather than being grounded in fact. We can give ourselves fresh options and chances to create riches by confronting and questioning these assumptions.

Consider the good effects that money can have in order to refute the assumption that it is the source of all evil. Money can be utilized to start businesses, fund philanthropic endeavors, and raise everyone's standard of living. We can start to perceive money as an instrument for good transformation and personal development if we reframe our attitudes.

8.1.3 Fostering a Mindset of Abundance

Developing an abundant mindset is a necessary step in changing our financial mindset. The idea that there is more than enough money and opportunity for everyone is known as an abundant mindset. It is the conviction that there is boundless opportunity for financial achievement and that we live in a rich universe.

It's critical to emphasize thankfulness and appreciation for what we already have in order to develop an abundant attitude. We may attract more wealth and opportunity into our lives by changing our perspective from one of scarcity to one of plenty. Maintaining a gratitude diary or consistently expressing your thankfulness for the wealth and abundance that are already a part of your life are two ways to cultivate gratitude.

8.1.4 Accepting Wealth as a Desired Outcome

It's critical to accept riches as a desirable objective in order to change our financial perspective. Many of us have been taught to think that wishing to be wealthy is self-centered or greedy. Wealth is neither intrinsically good nor bad, though. It is merely a tool that we can utilize to improve both our own and other people's lives.

We can get over any shame or guilt we may have about pursuing financial success by accepting riches as a desirable objective. We can decide on specific financial objectives and act with inspiration to accomplish them. Remember that building an abundant, free, and fulfilled life is just as important to riches as hoarding money.

8.1.5 Assembling a Positive Social Circle

The people in our social circles have a big impact on our thinking. We need to surround ourselves with supportive people who share our aims and desires if we want to change the way we think about money. Look for like-minded people who have succeeded financially and can serve as mentors, coaches, or sources of inspiration and guidance.

Furthermore, exercise caution when consuming information and media. Make sure you are surrounded by empowering and upbeat messages about achievement and money. Get inspired to think positively and abundantly by reading books, listening to podcasts, and attending seminars. We may maintain our motivation on the path to financial achievement by reinforcing our new money thinking and surrounding ourselves with good people.

8.1.6 Acting and Putting Change into Practice

Changing our financial attitude involves more than just altering our ideas and opinions; it also entails acting and bringing about change in our daily lives. Establishing definite financial objectives and devising a strategy to reach them is crucial. Learn about investment, wealth building, and money management to start your journey towards financial literacy.

Make a budget and keep track of your spending first. Create a savings plan and set up an automated savings system. Learn about the various investing options available to you and begin accumulating wealth through astute investments. Be open to new prospects for financial progress and take appropriate risks.

Recall that changing your financial perspective is a journey that calls for dedication and constant work. Treat yourself with kindness, and acknowledge your little victories as you go. Riches and abundance will start to come into your life as you keep changing your financial perspective. Accept the process and have fun while you develop a wealth mindset that will enable you to succeed financially and lead an abundant life.

8.2 Fostering Financial Knowledge

It is imperative that everyone have financial literacy, regardless of their financial objectives. It serves as the cornerstone around which wealth is created and maintained. Gaining an awareness of investment techniques, money management concepts, and the general operations of the financial industry is necessary for developing financial literacy. This section will discuss the value of financial literacy and offer doable strategies for enhancing this crucial ability.

8.2.1 Knowing the Fundamentals

It's critical to understand the foundational ideas of financial literacy before delving into its complexity. This entails comprehending the ideas of earnings, outlays, saving, and budgeting. The term "income" describes the money you make from investments, a business, or a paycheck. Contrarily, expenses are the out-of-pocket costs associated with living, like rent, utilities, groceries, and entertainment.

The practice of allocating your money to various spending and savings objectives is known as budgeting. You can use it to keep tabs on your expenses, find places where you can make savings, and make sure you are setting up enough money for the future. Setting aside money for investments, long-term financial objectives, and emergencies is the act of saving.

8.2.2 Learning for Yourself

Learning about different financial concepts and methods is crucial for developing financial literacy. You can accomplish this by reading books, going to seminars, enrolling in online courses, or consulting financial consultants. Learn the definitions of common financial words, such as retirement accounts, stocks, bonds, and mutual funds, before you begin.

Gaining knowledge about the world of money can be achieved through reading books authored by financial specialists. Seek out books on subjects like money development, investing, and personal finance. A few books that are suggested are "The Millionaire Next Door" by Thomas J. Stanley, "The Intelligent Investor" by Benjamin Graham, and "Rich Dad, Poor Dad" by Robert Kiyosaki.

Increasing your financial literacy can also be accomplished by participating in seminars and workshops organized by financial professionals. A wide range of subjects, such as wealth management, tax planning, and investment techniques, are frequently covered at these gatherings. Furthermore, you may learn about finance from the comfort of your home with the help of online courses and webinars, which are accessible and convenient options.

8.2.3 Creating Budgetary Objectives

Having specific financial goals and fostering financial literacy go hand in hand. It's challenging to make wise financial decisions when you don't have a clear goal in mind. Establish your short-, medium-, and long-term financial objectives first. While medium-term objectives can include saving for a down payment on a home or paying for a child's education, short-term objectives might include setting up an emergency fund or paying off debt. Planning for retirement or leaving a legacy for future generations are examples of long-term objectives.

Once your objectives have been determined, divide them into manageable steps. Calculate the monthly amount that you must invest or save in order to reach your objectives within the anticipated time frame. This will assist you in setting up a reasonable budget and allocating your resources appropriately.

8.2.4 Handling Debt

Effective debt management is one facet of financial literacy that is frequently disregarded. A major barrier to achieving financial independence and building wealth might be debt. It's critical to comprehend the various forms of debt, including mortgages, student loans, and credit card debt, and to create effective payment plans for each.

Examine your present debt status first. List all of your debts, together with the interest rate, minimum payment required each month, and outstanding balance. Paying off high-interest debt should be your top priority because it can mount up quickly and impede your financial success. To speed up your debt payback, take into account techniques like the debt avalanche or snowball methods.

8.2.5 Assembling a Portfolio of Investments

A vital part of wealth growth and financial literacy is investing. It entails investing your money in a variety of assets in an effort to get a return. A thorough awareness of the various investment possibilities, risk management, and diversification are necessary while building an investment portfolio.

Commence by familiarizing oneself with various investing vehicles, including stocks, bonds, mutual funds, property, and commodities. Recognize the possible risks and rewards connected to each asset class. Think about collaborating with a financial advisor who can assist you in creating an investment plan that takes into account your time horizon, financial objectives, and risk tolerance.

An essential component of creating an investment portfolio is diversification. To lower risk, it entails distributing your investments throughout several industries and asset types. You can lessen the effects of market swings and raise the possibility of long-term, steady profits by diversifying your portfolio.

8.2.6 Keeping Up-to-Date and Adjusting

Being financially literate takes constant effort and is not a one-time accomplishment. Since the financial industry is always changing, it's critical to keep up with the newest developments in terms of laws, regulations, and investment opportunities. Keep up with economic news, follow reliable financial websites, and subscribe to financial periodicals.

Furthermore, be flexible enough to modify your financial plans as needed. Regularly review your financial objectives and make any necessary adjustments. When in doubt, consult financial experts for guidance, and keep learning about fresh approaches and chances for investing.

You give yourself the power to create money, make wise financial decisions, and reach your financial objectives by becoming financially literate. It is a journey that lasts a lifetime and calls for constant learning and adjustment. Accept the process, remain dedicated to learning about finance, and observe how your financial future develops.

8.3 Prudent Investing

One essential habit that millionaires have perfected on their way to success is prudent investing. Creating money is not the only goal; you also need to make your money work for you. In order to help you make wise investment decisions and increase your wealth, we will examine the concepts and methods used by billionaires in this part.

8.3.1 Recognizing the Fundamentals of Investing

Gaining a fundamental understanding of investing is crucial before venturing further. Investing is distributing your funds among various assets in the hopes of earning a return over time. The secret is to strike a balance between return and risk, making sure that your investments match your risk tolerance and financial objectives.

Diversity: Dividing Your Hazard
Diversification is one of the cornerstones of prudent investing. Billionaires are aware of how important it is to diversify their holdings. They reduce the possibility of losing everything in the event that one investment underperforms by distributing their assets over a variety of asset classes, industries, and geographical areas. Investment portfolios that are more diverse can be more resilient and steady.

Time Horizon: Making Long-Term Investments
Billionaires approach investing with an eye toward the long term. They are aware that the market moves in cycles and that they shouldn't let temporary swings stop them from sticking to their investing plan. They can withstand market turbulence and get the benefits of compounding gains over time by concentrating on long-term objectives.

Risk Management: Evaluating and Reducing Hazards
Risk-aware investors, not risk-averse ones, are successful investors. They take precautions to reduce the risks involved in each investment after carefully evaluating them. They study market trends, carry out in-depth research, and consult experts when needed. Billionaires can reduce possible losses and make well-informed judgments by being aware of the dangers.

8.3.2 Billionaires' Investing Methods
Billionaires use a variety of financial techniques to increase their fortune. Let's look at a few of their tactics and see how you may incorporate them into your own investing process.

Value Investing: Finding Assets at a Discount
Finding undervalued assets and making investments in them with the hope that their value will rise over time is known as value investing. This is a tactic that billionaires like Warren

Buffett have perfected, concentrating on businesses with solid foundations and room to develop in the long run. Through comprehensive investigation and evaluation, they are able to pinpoint chances that others would miss.

Investing in High-Growth Enterprises: Growth Investing
Investing in businesses with the potential for rapid growth in the future is known as growth investing. Billionaires are aware of the potential of innovation, and they actively seek out businesses that are reshaping markets and sectors. They search for businesses with a history of steady growth, good leadership, and a competitive edge. Billionaires can reap significant financial rewards from their investments by making high-growth company investments.

Real Estate: Using Property to Build Wealth
For billionaires, real estate is a preferred investment option. They understand that real estate has the ability to provide both passive income and long-term appreciation. Billionaires make calculated real estate investments to diversify their holdings and provide steady cash flow, whether they be in the form of land, buildings, or homes. To help them make wise investment decisions, they draw on their expertise in location analysis, market trends, and property value.

Alternative Investments: Identifying Novel Prospects
Billionaires aren't hesitant to look at alternatives to conventional stocks and bonds as investments. They make investments in commodities, hedge funds, private equity, and venture capital, among other assets. Although they carry greater risks, these alternative investments have the potential for larger returns. Billionaires divide up their portfolio to diversify their assets after carefully weighing the benefits and hazards of each investment.

8.3.3 Getting Expert Counsel
Even though billionaires frequently have extensive knowledge of investment, they also appreciate the need for expert counsel.

They surround themselves with a group of accountants, lawyers, and financial consultants who offer professional advice and assist them in making difficult investment decisions. These experts are capable of managing risks, spotting opportunities, and maximizing investment plans because of their training and experience. Getting professional assistance may be quite beneficial, particularly for those who are just starting out in investing or don't have the time or knowledge to handle their money well.

8.3.4 Maintaining Knowledge and Adjusting to Market Shifts
Billionaires know how important it is to keep up with market developments and modify their investment plans accordingly. They keep themselves informed about economic statistics, read financial journals, and keep up with the latest advancements in the financial industry. They can see new opportunities and modify their investment portfolios to take advantage of market shifts by remaining informed. In order to make sure that their investments are in line with the constantly shifting dynamics of the market, they also have to be adaptable and willing to change course when necessary.

8.3.5 Controlling Feelings and Steering Clear of Impulsive Choices
To invest sensibly, one must control one's emotions and refrain from making snap judgments. Billionaires know how important it is to continue to approach investment with reason and discipline. They don't let greed or fear influence their investing choices. Rather, they depend on in-depth examination, investigation, and an extended viewpoint. Billionaires are able to make unbiased decisions that complement their financial goals and tactics by controlling their emotions.

In summary
One essential habit that millionaires have perfected on their path to wealth is prudent investing. You may make wise financial decisions and increase your wealth over time by

remaining informed, managing your emotions, using tried-and-true investment strategies, consulting a professional, and grasping the fundamentals of investing. Recall that investing is a long-term endeavor, and attaining financial success requires discipline, patience, and a well-thought-out plan.

8.4: Creating Several Revenue Streams

One characteristic that unites billionaires around the globe and makes them stand out from the others is their capacity to produce several sources of income. While the majority of people only have one source of income, billionaires know how important it is to diversify their assets and open up new opportunities to build wealth. Creating several revenue streams offers prospects for wealth building and exponential growth in addition to financial security.

8.4.1 Diversification's Power

One of the most important concepts in creating several revenue streams is diversification. It entails distributing your assets and revenue streams among several marketplaces, asset classes, and industry sectors. Billionaires reduce risk and make sure that they are not reliant on any one source of income by diversifying. They can take advantage of different chances and adjust to shifting market conditions thanks to this technique.

8.4.2 Real Estate Investing

Real estate is a well-liked means of creating several revenue sources. Billionaires see the benefit of making investments in real estate that increase in value or produce passive income through capital gains or rental revenue. They make use of their financial resources to buy industrial, commercial, or residential properties in order to generate a consistent flow of rental income. To further diversify their real estate holdings, they could potentially venture into property development or real estate investment trusts (REITs).

8.4.3 Business ventures and entrepreneurship
Billionaires frequently possess a strong sense of entrepreneurship and a talent for spotting profitable business ventures. They establish and invest in companies in a variety of industries by utilizing their knowledge, contacts, and financial resources. Having numerous enterprises allows them to benefit from the potential growth and scalability of these endeavors in addition to generating revenue. To focus on new projects and prospects, successful businesspeople know how important it is to assemble a solid team and assign tasks to others.

8.4.4 Investing in the Stock Market
Another strategy used by billionaires to create several revenue sources is stock market investing. To make wise investment selections, they closely examine economic statistics, corporate performance, and market trends. Billionaires can make money from dividends, capital gains, and interest payments by carefully building a diverse portfolio of stocks, bonds, and other financial instruments. In order to optimize profits and reduce risks, they frequently collaborate closely with financial consultants and investment specialists.

8.4.5 Royalties and Intellectual Property
Billionaires are aware of the importance of intellectual property and how royalties may be used to create passive income. They can produce and grant licenses for trade secrets, copyrights, trademarks, and patents so they can profit from the usage of their intellectual property. Royalties from movies, software, music, books, and even business strategies that are franchised can fall under this category. Billionaires are able to continue making money long after they make their original investment or creation by using their imagination and inventiveness.

8.4.6 Venture Capital and Startup Investments
In order to diversify their sources of income and take advantage of opportunities with significant growth potential, billionaires frequently invest in startups and venture capital

funds. They offer early-stage enterprises funding, knowledge, and mentoring in return for shares or a cut of the business's future profits. Billionaires can profit from the rapid expansion and success of these businesses by investing in a portfolio of startups, possibly yielding large returns on their capital.

8.4.7 Interest and Dividends as Passive Income

Billionaires are aware of the potential of interest and dividend payments as sources of passive income. To generate a consistent flow of cash, they make investments in stocks, bonds, and other income-producing assets that pay dividends. Over time, they can compound their wealth by reinvesting these returns. To generate interest on their cash, billionaires can also invest in peer-to-peer lending platforms, certificates of deposit (CDs), and high-yield savings accounts.

8.4.8 Online Stores and Online Shopping

Since the internet has grown in popularity, billionaires have taken advantage of the opportunity to create several revenue streams through e-commerce and online enterprises. They reach a large consumer base by selling goods and services globally via the use of technology and digital platforms. Billionaires are familiar with the scalability and profitability of online businesses, whether they are in software development, dropshipping, affiliate marketing, e-books, or online courses.

8.4.9 Franchising and Licensing

Billionaires use franchising and licensing as ways to increase their revenue streams without having to make large capital investments. In return for royalties or franchise fees, they grant licenses to other companies or people to use their brand, goods, or services. This enables them to control their intellectual property and brand reputation while making use of other people's talents and abilities to create revenue.

8.4.10 Charitable Investing

Billionaires understand the value of changing the world and giving back to the community. They might put money into foundations, social enterprises, or charitable endeavors that share their objectives and ideals. Even though these investments might not yield immediate financial gains, billionaires benefit from them in terms of fulfillment and purpose, as well as beneficial social effects.

It takes a combination of financial know-how, strategic thinking, and a willingness to take calculated risks to build several streams of income. It is a long-term strategy for creating money rather than a fast fix. Billionaires secure their financial security, generate growth prospects, and eventually attain the financial independence that permits them to lead independent lives by spreading their revenue streams.

PRACTICING DISCIPLINE AND CONSISTENCY

9.1 Clearly Delineating Boundaries
Billionaires have learned the importance of setting boundaries in order to stay focused and productive and maintain a healthy balance in their lives. They may safeguard their time, energy, and resources by setting limits, which enable them to remain focused on their objectives and keep away from pointless distractions. This section will discuss the value of establishing boundaries and offer doable tactics for putting them into practice in your own life.

The Value of Establishing Limits
In order to avoid burnout and maintain a healthy work-life balance, setting boundaries is crucial. Billionaires know that their time and energy are precious assets that should be safeguarded. They are able to efficiently distribute their resources and prioritize their responsibilities by establishing defined boundaries.

Establishing boundaries enables people to concentrate on their most crucial responsibilities and objectives, which is one of its main advantages. Setting limits gives you a framework that keeps you focused and prevents you from getting distracted by unimportant tasks. This makes it possible for you to move closer to your objectives in a more effective and efficient manner.

Setting limits also makes it easier to communicate your requirements to others and create expectations. You may establish a foundation for positive interactions and relationships by outlining exactly what is and is not acceptable. This can help avoid miscommunications, confrontations, and needless tension.

Techniques for Defined Boundaries
Now that we know how important it is to set boundaries, let's look at some doable methods for putting them into practice in your own life:

1. Determine what your top priorities are.

Setting boundaries requires that you first decide what your priorities are. Spend some time thinking about your priorities and the goals you have for both your personal and professional lives. This will assist you in deciding where to set boundaries and where to spend your time and energy.

2. Express Your Limitations

After you've determined your priorities, it's critical to let people know what your boundaries are. Make it clear to others what you expect from them and what you will and won't do. This can be accomplished by having direct and honest discussions, outlining expectations, and creating ground rules that both parties can agree upon.

3. Develop your ability to refuse.

One important talent that billionaires have mastered is saying no. It's critical to understand that you are not able to do everything and that turning down offers or requests that conflict with your objectives or values is acceptable. Remember that saying no is not a reflection of your value or competence, and practice saying no in an authoritative and courteous manner.

4. Place Technological and Distraction Limits

It's easy to become distracted by technology and continual diversions in the digital age we live in. Billionaires recognize the value of establishing boundaries and restrictions on the use of technology. Think about creating areas off-limits to technology or setting aside specific hours to check social media and emails. This will assist you in maintaining your attention and presence during the most important jobs and activities.

5. Guard your time.

Billionaires know how important it is to safeguard their limited time. Allocate a specific time for your top priorities and objectives, and zealously protect that time. Reduce distractions, assign work when you can, and plan your time so that you have time for both personal and concentrated work.

6. Take care of yourself.

Taking care of yourself entails setting boundaries as well. Make self-care activities a priority, including hobbies, rest, and exercise. Making time for self-care helps you stay mentally and energetically refreshed, which improves your general wellbeing and productivity.

7. Assess and modify

Establishing limits is a continuous process. Make sure your boundaries are still fulfilling your needs and priorities by periodically evaluating them. To make sure your boundaries continue to promote your professional and personal development, be willing to tweak and improve them as necessary.

In summary

One essential habit that millionaires have learned to perfect in order to succeed in life is setting clear limits. Setting limits helps you maintain balance, productivity, and focus by safeguarding your time, energy, and resources. By putting the tactics covered in this section into practice, you will have the ability to establish limits and build a framework for both professional and personal development. Recall that establishing limits is an essential step in reaching your objectives and leading a satisfying life, not a sign of selfishness.

9.2 Remaining Devoted to Objectives

A key to success in any effort is maintaining commitment to goals. It is the capacity to endure in the face of difficulties and disappointments and to keep one's eyes on the goal. This part will look at the routines and tactics used by billionaires to stay dedicated to their objectives, which helps them get over challenges and produce amazing outcomes.

9.2.1 Specify Your Objectives

Clearly defining your objectives is the first step in maintaining your commitment to them. The capacity to create clear, ambitious goals that support their vision and principles is a hallmark of billionaires. Spend some time carefully defining your objectives, making sure they are time-bound, meaningful, measurable, and reachable. By making your objectives clear, you build a road map for your actions and maintain focus on the intended result.

9.2.2 Formulate an Alluring Vision

It is crucial to have an inspiring and motivating vision if you want to remain dedicated to your goals. Billionaires frequently see their goals as already completed because they recognize the power of vision. You can use the power of your subconscious mind to propel you to take persistent action toward your goals by seeing your ideal outcome in vivid detail. Reminding yourself of your goals and the reasons you want to attain them on a regular basis helps strengthen your resolve and commitment.

9.2.3 Organize Your Objectives

Billionaires know that having lofty objectives can be demotivating and cause a lack of dedication. They divide their objectives into more doable, smaller activities in order to get around this. Your motivation and devotion are fueled when you break down your goals into manageable chunks and feel like you're making progress. Celebrate every accomplishment along the way since it will serve to reaffirm your dedication and inspire you to keep going.

9.2.4 Create a Safety Net

A support network is essential for maintaining your commitment to your objectives. Assemble a support system of like-minded people who can inspire and motivate you to pursue your goals. Look for instructors or mentors who have accomplished the goals you seek for yourself. You can overcome obstacles and stay on course with their advice and experience. In addition, think about connecting with people who share your commitment to success and personal development by joining mastermind groups or communities.

9.2.5 Exercise Self-Control

One essential habit that billionaires develop to maintain their commitment to their objectives is self-discipline. It is the capacity to restrain your desires, maintain focus, and continuously move toward your objectives—even in the face of difficulty or inconvenience. Create regular rituals and routines that help you achieve your objectives and get rid of distractions that could impede your development. Exercise self-control and arrange your duties in order of importance and fit with your objectives. You may boost your chances of success and solidify your commitment by continuously exercising self-discipline.

9.2.6 Remain Responsible
Accountability is a useful tool for maintaining your commitment to your objectives. Billionaires know how important it is to take responsibility for oneself and others. Set up mechanisms to monitor your development and ensure that you consistently take action. Tell those you can trust to support and hold you accountable about your goals. Think about joining a mastermind group or finding an accountability partner so you can discuss your progress and check in on a regular basis. Maintaining accountability helps you develop a sense of accountability and strengthens your will to reach your objectives.

9.2.7 Accept Adaptability and Flexibility
As important as it is to stick to your course, it's just as important to be adaptive and flexible. Success rarely follows a straight line, and obstacles like setbacks and unforeseen difficulties are unavoidable. Billionaires know how important it is to be flexible and change course when necessary. Keep an open mind and be prepared to shift course if things need to. Accepting flexibility helps you stay true to your objectives and be adaptable to the constantly shifting surroundings.

9.2.8 Develop an optimistic outlook
A positive outlook is essential for maintaining your commitment to your objectives. Billionaires are aware of the influence that positive thinking has on their dedication and drive. Practice gratitude, affirmations, and visualization to foster a good outlook. Get rid of your limiting thoughts and negative self-talk, and surround yourself with good influences. You can become more resilient and committed to reaching your goals in the face of hardship by keeping an optimistic outlook.

9.2.9 Evaluate and Modify
Make sure your objectives and achievements are still in line with your vision and values by reviewing them on a regular

basis. As you develop and mature, it could be necessary to modify or enhance your objectives. Reevaluating your objectives and making the required adjustments will help you stay true to what really matters to you. Consider your accomplishments and draw lessons from any mistakes or losses. Make the most of these encounters to advance your development. You can stay committed and make sure you're headed in the correct direction by regularly assessing and tweaking your goals.

9.2.10 Remain Motivated

Lastly, you need a continuous source of inspiration to stay dedicated to your goals. Look for motivational speakers, podcasts, or publications that speak to you personally as inspiration. Keep yourself inspired and motivated by surrounding yourself with good and encouraging stuff that reaffirms your commitment. Review your vision often and keep in mind the positive effects that reaching your objectives will have on both your life and the lives of others. You can sustain your dedication and the motivation to work tirelessly toward your goals by continuing to be inspired.

In conclusion, a key component of success is maintaining your commitment to your objectives. You can cultivate the commitment required to achieve extraordinary results by being clear about what you want to achieve, coming up with a compelling vision, breaking it down, building a support system, exercising self-discipline, being accountable, accepting flexibility, adopting a positive mindset, reviewing and making adjustments, and remaining inspired. If you follow the routines and approaches used by billionaires, you will be well on your way to reaching your objectives and leading a prosperous and satisfying life.

9.3 Establishing Daily Schedules

Creating regular routines is essential to success and to living a successful and meaningful life. Billionaires know the value of routines and how they keep them motivated, focused, and well-organized. This section will discuss the significance of creating daily routines and offer helpful advice on how to design routines that support your objectives.

9.3.1 The Advantages of Everyday Habits

Our lives are given shape and stability by our daily routines. They allow us to maximize our time and energy and assist us in establishing a sense of order. Routines for billionaires are about more than just getting things done; they're about making the most of their abilities and performance. The following are some of the main advantages of creating daily routines:

Enhanced Output

Billionaires are able to effectively manage their time and prioritize their duties by adhering to a regimen. This enables them to concentrate on worthwhile endeavors that advance their long-term objectives. Routines prevent decision fatigue and help billionaires make decisions quickly and wisely, which boosts output.

Better Organization of Time

Billionaires recognize the value of time as a resource and the significance of efficiently allocating it. Daily routines assist individuals in setting aside time for particular tasks, making sure they allot enough time for their personal, professional, and self-care obligations. Billionaires may maximize their time and prevent squandering it on pointless activities by adhering to a regimented schedule.

Improved attention and focus

Billionaires find that sticking to a daily schedule helps them avoid distractions and stay focused on their top goals. By setting out separate time slots for various tasks, people can focus on jobs that demand their complete attention and devote uninterrupted hours to in-depth work. They are able to generate better work and reach greater production levels as a result.

Decreased Overwhelm and Stress
Billionaires frequently have hectic lives with lots of duties. They can lessen stress and overwhelm by adhering to a regular schedule, which helps them better manage their time and responsibilities. The sense of control and certainty that routines offer helps millionaires face each day with a cool, collected head.

Maintaining order and discipline
Everyday rituals help billionaires live lives that are consistent and disciplined. By sticking to a schedule, they form habits that help them achieve their objectives. Long-term success requires consistency, and billionaires find that rituals keep them focused on their goals even in the face of obstacles or disappointments.

9.3.2 Creating a Productive Daily Schedule
Planning and thought go into developing a successful daily schedule. It ought to be customized to your unique objectives, tastes, and way of life. To assist you in creating a schedule that suits you, consider the following steps:

Determine your top priorities.
Determine your priorities and the activities that will help you achieve your objectives first. Which are the most crucial things you have to get done every day? Knowing what your priorities are will help you organize your routine so that time and energy are spent appropriately.

Establish specific objectives.
Having specific objectives is necessary to create a routine that works. Establish your goals for yourself in terms of your work, health, relationships, and personal development. Activities that advance these objectives and aid in your routine should be a part of it.

Set aside time blocks.
Your day should be divided into time blocks, with designated activities for each block. You may set aside time in the morning for concentrated work, in the afternoon for pleasure and relaxation, and in the morning for exercise and self-care.

Make sure you plan enough time for breaks and transitions and estimate each task's time realistically.

Set high-value activities first.
Concentrate on high-value pursuits that will significantly advance your objectives. Determine which of your routine's duties are most important to your success and give them top priority. By doing this, you'll be able to move closer to your top priorities and stay away from time-wasting or low-value pursuits.

Included Flexibility
Routines offer structure, but it's crucial to have some wiggle room to account for unforeseen circumstances or shifting priorities. Make time in your schedule to deal with unforeseen events or seize unplanned chances. Being flexible lets you change with the times without being stressed out or overwhelmed.

Review and modify frequently.
Make sure your routine is still in line with your priorities and goals by reviewing it on a regular basis. You might need to modify your routine as your circumstances change to make room for new commitments or goals. To maximize your productivity and well-being, be willing to try out new strategies and adjust your regimen.

9.3.3 Advice for Keeping Up Your Daily Schedule
It's crucial to stick to your daily schedule once you've created an efficient one. Here are some pointers to keep you on course:

Begin small and gain speed.
If you're not experienced in creating daily routines, begin with little, doable adjustments. To gain momentum, gradually include new routines and activities. By starting modest, you can avoid overwhelm and enhance the likelihood that you will stick to your habit.

Establish Accountability

Seek methods for keeping oneself responsible for adhering to your schedule. Talk about your objectives and advancement with a family member or close friend who you can rely on for encouragement and support. It is also possible to track your routine and get reminders by using technological tools or applications.

Remain dedicated and adaptable.
Discipline and dedication are needed to keep up a regular schedule. Reminding yourself of the advantages and successful results of sticking to your regimen will help you stay motivated. In addition, exercise flexibility and adaptability in the face of unforeseen circumstances. Recall that your routine should support your well-being and goals rather than impose strict constraints.

Honor accomplishments and make necessary adjustments.
Along the journey, acknowledge and appreciate your accomplishments. Acknowledge the improvements your routine has made in your life as well as the actions you have taken to get closer to your objectives. Be open to adjusting and trying new things if some parts of your schedule aren't working as planned. As you develop and alter, your routine should also vary.

Creating a daily routine is an effective habit that has the ability to change your life. You may improve your general well-being, productivity, and focus by creating and adhering to a routine that works for you. Recall that routines are tools that enable you to maximize your time and energy, not things designed to limit or constrain you. On the road to success, embrace the power of routines and realize your greatest potential.

9.4 Retaining Attention and Preventing Diversions
It's harder than ever to stay focused and avoid distractions in the fast-paced, always-connected world of today. Being able to maintain focus on our priorities and goals is essential for success, especially for those who want to become billionaires.

This section will examine the methods and approaches employed by billionaires to keep their attention and reduce outside distractions so they can be as productive as possible and accomplish their objectives.

9.4.1 Establishing a Space Free from Distractions

Establishing a distraction-free workplace is one of the first stages of staying focused. Billionaires know how important it is to have a private area where they can work uninterrupted. This might be a personal workstation at their workplace, a calm area in a coffee shop, or an office at home. They do this by getting rid of outside distractions like noise, clutter, and interruptions and by creating an atmosphere that encourages focus and production.

In order to eliminate distractions, millionaires frequently use strategies like:

Reducing noise: To reduce outside noise and foster a peaceful, concentrated environment, they either play instrumental music or wear noise-canceling headphones.

Keeping their workspace organized: They make sure that everything they need is conveniently available and within reach by keeping their workspace neat and free of clutter.

Boundaries: They communicate their desire for unbroken work time to friends, family, and coworkers by establishing clear boundaries.

9.4.2 Meditation and Mindfulness Practices

Billionaires employ strong tools like mindfulness and meditation to train their minds and improve their capacity to stay focused. They get the knowledge to spot distractions when they happen and the self-control to bring their focus back to the activity at hand by engaging in mindfulness practices.

Billionaires frequently include mindfulness and meditation in their daily regimens, setting aside a short period of time for introspection and mental clarity. Through the cultivation of a calm and concentrated mentality, this exercise facilitates their ability to effectively navigate through many distractions.

9.4.3 Setting Priorities and Scheduling Time

Setting priorities for their work and setting time limits are two other crucial techniques used by billionaires to keep their attention. They are aware that not every task is equal and that some actions will affect their aims more than others. Billionaires make sure they are focusing their efforts and energy on the things that will have the biggest impact on their lives by determining what their most crucial responsibilities are and setting out specific time blocks for them.

Billionaires frequently employ strategies like:

The Matrix of Eisenhower: They prioritize work efficiently and concentrate on high-value activities by dividing them into four quadrants according to their urgency and importance.
Time blocking: They set aside particular blocks of time for various kinds of work, including meetings, creative work, and administrative duties. By designating specific time windows for every task, they reduce the likelihood of becoming distracted or overburdened.

9.4.4 Putting Digital Detox in Place

When it comes to focusing in the modern digital age, technology may be both a help and a hindrance. It offers us countless chances to be productive and connected, but it also offers a plethora of distractions that can cause us to lose concentration and become less productive.

Billionaires understand how important it is to take occasional breaks from technology in order to refocus and recharge. They put digital detoxes into practice by:

Establishing boundaries: They designate certain periods during the day, such as meals, right before bed, or during concentrated work sessions, when they will not be using their gadgets.
Using productivity applications: During set work intervals, they use productivity apps to prevent access to social media, email, and other distracting websites.

Designating "tech-free zones": They set apart spaces in their houses or workplaces where using electronics is prohibited, creating a haven for unhindered work or leisure.

9.4.5 The Art of Single-Tasking

Despite what many people think, multitasking is not a quality of highly successful people. Billionaires are aware that multitasking really lowers productivity and the caliber of work produced. Rather, they engage in single-tasking, dedicating all of their concentration to a single task.

Billionaires are able to reach a state of flow, where they work at their best and are deeply concentrated, by giving one task their entire focus. They are able to do high-quality work faster because they resist the need to jump between activities or reply to every notification that comes in.

9.4.6 Developing Self-Control

It all boils down to developing self-discipline to keep focused and avoid distractions. Billionaires know that self-control is a muscle that requires constant exercise. They hold themselves responsible for their objectives and pledges, and they form routines and habits that enhance their concentration and productivity.

In order to develop self-control, millionaires frequently:

Establish defined objectives: They make a plan that directs their actions and choices by precisely defining their objectives.

Practice delaying gratification: They are prepared to give up short-term gratification and diversions in order to achieve long-term success.

Celebrate little victories. They encourage themselves to keep focused by rewarding themselves for reaching milestones and staying on task. This helps them stay motivated and focused.

Billionaires are able to resist the draw of side trips and remain focused on their objectives in the face of difficulties or temptations because they have developed self-control.

In summary

Success in every activity requires the ability to stay focused and avoid distractions. Billionaires are able to increase their productivity and produce remarkable outcomes by establishing a distraction-free atmosphere, exercising mindfulness, prioritizing tasks, putting digital detoxes into place, practicing single-tasking, and developing self-discipline. By implementing these tactics and methods, readers can also improve their capacity for maintaining attention and reducing outside distractions, which will help them on their way to success. Recall that staying focused is a constant activity that calls for dedication and self-control, rather than an isolated endeavor. Everyone may adopt the habits of millionaires and reach their full potential if they are determined and persistent enough.

EMBRACING CONTINUOUS LEARNING

10.1 Lifelong Learning's Power

One essential characteristic that separates millionaires from the rest is their commitment to lifelong learning. They are aware that information is power and that success and personal development depend on lifelong learning. In this chapter, we will examine the potential of lifelong learning and how it can change your life.

10.1.1 The Advantages of Continuous Education

Acquiring knowledge is only one aspect of lifelong learning; another is adopting a growth-oriented and inquisitive mindset. Billionaires are aware that there is always something new to learn and that education is a lifetime endeavor. The following are a few advantages to lifelong learning:

1. Individual Development and Progress

You can grow yourself by expanding your knowledge and skill set through lifelong learning. It lets you take advantage of fresh chances and maintain your relevance in a world that is changing quickly. You may improve your skills, widen your horizons, and reach your greatest potential by never stopping learning.

2. Flexibility and Sturdiness

Adaptability is essential in the fast-paced, constantly-changing environment we live in today. You can adjust to new difficulties and situations with the information and abilities you gain through lifelong learning. It supports the growth of resilience and the self-assurance needed to move through adversity. Accepting lifelong learning makes you more adaptable and better able to survive in any setting.

3. Career Promotion

Success in the workplace is largely dependent on ongoing learning. It makes it possible for you to learn new skills, stay ahead of the curve, and compete in the employment market. Investing in your own personal development raises your worth as an employee or business owner. Opportunities for new company ventures, job improvements, and promotions might arise from pursuing lifelong learning.

4. Stimulation of the Mind

Learning maintains mental acuity and focus. It sharpens your mind, develops your cognitive functions, and strengthens your memory. You are forced to solve puzzles, think critically, and discover new concepts through lifelong learning. It ensures a full and active life by keeping your brain engaged and preventing cognitive decline.

5. Self-Realization

The process of learning is incredibly rewarding and enriching. It enables you to follow worthwhile projects, explore your passions, and pick up new interests. By giving one a sense of purpose and achievement, lifelong learning promotes personal fulfillment. It enables you to consistently develop and grow as a person, which results in a life that is more meaningful and gratifying.

10.1.2 Lifelong Learning Techniques

Now that we are aware of how important lifelong learning is, let's look at some ways you can apply it to your everyday activities:

1. Read a Variety of Books

One of the best ways to broaden your horizons and learn new things is to read. Develop the habit of reading a wide range of books. Investigate many genres, subjects, and viewpoints. Read thought-provoking books, articles, and blogs to broaden your horizons and sharpen your intellect. Make reading a priority in your life and set aside time for it every day.

2. Look for role models and mentors.

It is priceless to gain knowledge from successful people. Look for mentors and role models who can help you along the way and motivate you. Take note of their behaviors and mindset, ask for guidance, and learn from their experiences. Be in the company of others who share your commitment to accomplishment and personal development.

3. Go to seminars and workshops.

Attending conferences, seminars, and workshops is an investment in your own development. These gatherings offer chances to pick up fresh insights, network with like-minded people, and learn from professionals in a variety of industries. Benefit from the flexibility and convenience that online courses and webinars provide while you pursue your education.

4. Adopt virtual learning environments.

The way we learn has been transformed by the internet. Benefit from the many courses available on online learning platforms covering a variety of areas. These platforms give you the freedom to learn at your own speed, access to knowledgeable professors, and interactive course materials. Welcome to technology as a resource for continuous education.

5. Record and consider what you've learned.

Maintain a notebook or record your education. Jot down your learning experiences' most important lessons, realizations, and observations. Review and consider what you have learned on a regular basis, and note any areas that still require improvement. Your grasp of the subjects you study will be strengthened and deepened with the aid of this exercise.

10.1.3 The Path to Ongoing Education

Lifelong learning is an ongoing process rather than a final destination. Adopt a lifetime learning attitude and make a commitment to your continued personal improvement. Keep in mind that learning is not restricted to formal education or life stages. It's a career-long endeavor that can improve all facets of your life.

You may realize your full potential, succeed in both your personal and professional lives, and have a purposeful and fulfilled existence by embracing the power of lifelong learning. Decide to put money into your own development and adopt a lifelong learning mindset. This is where the trip starts.

10.2 Reading and Getting Knowledge

One of the most important habits of billionaires and successful people is reading and learning new things. They are aware of the value of lifelong learning and how it can advance both their careers and personal lives. In this part, we will discuss the value of reading, how to make reading a habit, and various methods of knowledge acquisition.

10.2.1 The Influence of Reading

Reading is a great way to learn new things and further one's own development. Billionaires know that reading broadens their horizons, gives them new perspectives, and keeps them up-to-date on the newest concepts and trends. They can gain access to other people's knowledge and experiences through reading, take lessons from their triumphs and mistakes, and apply those lessons to their own lives.

Additionally, reading increases language and communication skills, sharpens critical thinking abilities, and stimulates the intellect. It creates a hunger for information, opens doors to new vistas, and ignites creativity. Billionaires get a competitive edge in their areas because they read a lot and are able to learn new things constantly.

10.2.2 Forming a Reading Routine

It's critical to form a regular reading habit if you want to profit from reading. The following techniques will assist you in developing this habit:

Allocate a certain time for reading: Set aside a certain period of time every day or week to read. Like any other significant assignment, give it top importance and make a commitment to it.

Establish a pleasant and peaceful reading location so that you can concentrate and fully immerse yourself in the book. Reduce outside distractions and establish a calm environment so that you can concentrate on the subject matter at hand.

Start with subjects you are interested in. Read books on subjects you are actually interested in. This will enhance your enjoyment of the reading process and inspire you to read more.

Establish reading objectives for yourself. Set a goal to finish a certain number of books or pages in a given amount of time. Having goals will enable you to monitor your development and maintain motivation.

Always keep a book on you. Whether it's an electronic book on your tablet or smartphone or a physical book, make it a habit to always carry a book with you. This way, you can read whenever you have some free time during the day, like while you're in line or during your commute.

Become a member of a reading or book club. Talking with people who like reading as much as you do might help you comprehend the subject matter better and introduce you to various viewpoints. It also offers a chance to network with people who share similar interests.

10.2.3 Methods for Gaining Information
Reading is only one way to learn new things. Billionaires realize how important it is to keep an eye out for fresh ways to broaden their knowledge base and to diversify their information sources. The following are some other methods for learning:

Attend seminars and conferences: By taking part in seminars and conferences, you can pick the brains of professionals from a variety of fields. It offers a chance to learn new things, connect with like-minded people, and keep current with business trends.

Seek out mentors and role models. They can share their experiences and knowledge while offering insightful advice. Seek out people who are successful in the fields you are interested in, and take note of their insights.

Participate in online education by making use of the many different online learning resources and courses that are offered. With the ease and flexibility these tools provide, you can study a variety of subjects and learn at your own pace.

Listen to podcasts and audiobooks. These mobile-friendly information sources are excellent for on-the-go learning. They give people access to talks, interviews, and insights from professionals in a range of disciplines.

Participate in reflective learning by giving your experiences some thought and drawing lessons from them. You can incorporate new knowledge into your life and obtain deeper insights by journaling, reflecting on your life, and practicing meditation.

Recall that becoming knowledgeable involves more than just gathering facts. It all comes down to putting what you've learned into practice and always looking for ways to get better. Your entire potential can be realized, and the path to success in all facets of your life can be paved with a love of reading and a lifelong learning mindset.

In summary
We discussed the value of reading and learning in this section as steps toward success. We talked about the value of reading, creating a reading habit, and methods for learning things outside of books. You may adopt the habits of billionaires and advance your career and personal development by prioritizing reading, looking for a variety of information sources, and adopting a lifelong learning mindset. Do not forget that information is power and that your potential increases with your level of knowledge. Thus, begin reading, continue to study, and let the knowledge you gain serve as the catalyst for your achievement.

10.3 Looking for Mentors and Emulations

A fundamental practice shared by billionaires is their dedication to looking for mentors and role models. They are aware of the value of taking advice from people who have already attained the degree of success they aim for. Billionaires can obtain insightful advice, helpful assistance, and encouragement from people who have gone before them, which helps hasten their own ascent to success.

10.3.1 The Significance of Guides

For billionaires, mentors are essential to their careers and personal growth. These are accomplished professionals who have attained great success in their industries and who are eager to impart their wisdom to others. Mentors assist billionaires in overcoming obstacles, making wise decisions, and avoiding typical errors by offering direction, encouragement, and insightful counsel based on their own experiences.

Billionaires who have a mentor have access to years' worth of knowledge and expertise that would otherwise be difficult to obtain. Mentors can offer insightful commentary on market trends, success tactics, and direction for both career and personal development. Additionally, they can serve as a sounding board for ideas, assisting billionaires in honing their goals and coming to more informed conclusions.

10.3.2 Selecting the Appropriate Mentor

One of the most important steps on the road to success is choosing the appropriate mentor. Billionaires know how important it is to select a partner who shares their values, ambitions, and goals. They look for mentors who have attained the degree of success they want and who exhibit the traits and abilities they hope to acquire.

Billionaires typically begin their search for the ideal mentor by locating people who have excelled in their sector or expertise. To make sure there is alignment, they look at their successes, history, and values. Professional associations, business conferences, and networking events are excellent venues for meeting possible mentors. Billionaires also make use of their current network and ask friends or trustworthy coworkers for advice.

Billionaires approach possible mentors with humility and respect once they have been identified. They thank their mentor for his or her accomplishments and explain why they think they could learn from them. Billionaires are prepared to devote time and energy to fostering a mentor-mentee relationship because they recognize that it takes two to tango.

10.3.3 Taking Advice from Models

Billionaires look up to role models who inspire and motivate them, in addition to looking for mentors. Those who have attained exceptional success and who exemplify the traits and principles that billionaires strive to imitate are considered role models. By demonstrating what is possible and encouraging billionaires to aim high, they act as a source of inspiration and motivation.

Billionaires research the lives and professions of their inspirations in an effort to comprehend the attitudes, routines, and methods that have facilitated their success. They examine their successes, setbacks, and decision-making procedures in order to derive important lessons that they might use in their own lives.

A wide range of professions and sectors can produce role models. They could be business owners, executives, sportsmen, artists, or benefactors. The most important thing is that billionaires identify with their principles, respect their achievements, and draw inspiration from their path.

10.3.4 Copying Achievement

Billionaires know that traces of success are left behind. They can spot trends and tactics that have aided in their success by examining the routines and behaviors of their mentors and role models. After that, they apply these teachings to their own lives, customizing them to fit their own objectives and set of circumstances.

It is not necessary to follow someone else's exact route in order to emulate accomplishment. Rather, billionaires incorporate what speaks to them into their lives in a way that is consistent with their goals and principles. The techniques and routines they pick up from their mentors and role models are modified and tailored to fit their own journeys.

Billionaires also know that success is a journey rather than a destination. As they advance in their own journey, they continue to be receptive to learning from others and actively seek out new mentors and role models. They know that there's always more to learn and that they can keep evolving and growing by drawing on the knowledge and experience of others.

In summary

One of the most effective habits that billionaires use to hasten their ascent to success is looking for mentors and role models. Billionaires get important ideas, direction, and support from those who have previously accomplished what they want to achieve, which helps accelerate their own progress. Billionaires are cognizant of the significance of lifelong learning and its potential to enhance their personal and professional growth, whether through studying the lives of successful individuals, seeking out the ideal mentor, or imitating their achievements. By making this a habit, readers can also benefit from the knowledge and expertise of others, hastening their own path to achievement and contentment.

10.4 Making Personal Growth Investments

One important characteristic that distinguishes millionaires from the rest is their investment in personal development. They know that they have to keep investing in their own growth and development if they want to succeed in the long run. This chapter examines the value of making an investment in one's own personal development and offers doable tactics that readers can use right away.

10.4.1 The Worth of Individual Development

Billionaires understand that personal development is a lifetime endeavor of self-improvement rather than merely gaining knowledge or abilities. They realize that the best investment they can make is in themselves, because doing so will pay off handsomely in every aspect of their lives. They can broaden their minds, acquire fresh viewpoints, and realize their greatest potential through personal growth.

Billionaires remain ahead of the curve in a world that is constantly changing by making investments in their personal development. They recognize that in order to take advantage of new business prospects, industry trends, and technological advancements, they must always be learning and improving. They adopt a continual learning mentality, continuously looking for fresh insights and opportunities to improve both their personal and professional lives.

10.4.2 Determining Your Own Growth Objectives

Establishing measurable objectives is essential for investing in personal development in an efficient manner. Billionaires utilize goal-setting as a guide for their personal growth because they recognize its power. They establish SMART goals—specific, measurable, realistic, relevant, and time-bound—in line with their mission and core principles.

Billionaires can better focus their efforts and monitor their development by establishing personal growth goals. They build actionable plans to accomplish their goals by breaking them down into smaller benchmarks. By establishing goals, people give their personal growth journey direction and purpose, which keeps them moving forward and improving all the time.

10.4.3 Accepting Lifelong Learning

Billionaires are dedicated to lifelong learning and have a ravenous desire for knowledge. They know that education isn't just about going to school; there are other ways to learn, such as through books, podcasts, online courses, seminars, and mentoring. They actively look for chances to increase their knowledge and abilities and push themselves to keep improving.

Billionaires frequently read because it gives them access to a plethora of knowledge and perspectives from the brightest minds in a variety of industries. They look for biographies, self-help books, and industry-specific literature, and they emphasize reading works that are pertinent to their career and personal development. They are able to see things from fresh angles, spark their imagination, and keep up with the newest advancements and trends by reading widely.

Billionaires look for mentors and role models who can help and motivate them on their personal development journey, in addition to reading. They are prepared to share their expertise and experiences because they recognize the importance of learning from others who have already succeeded. Mentors aid billionaires in overcoming obstacles and expediting their own personal development by offering insightful counsel, encouragement, and support.

10.4.4 Purchasing Resources for Personal Development

Billionaires are aware that making financial investments is

frequently necessary to engage in personal development. They are prepared to spend money on conferences, seminars, and workshops that will advance their knowledge and abilities. They understand that these are long-term investments in themselves and their future prosperity rather than one-time costs.

Billionaires invest in resources and tools for personal growth in addition to going to events. They might employ consultants or coaches to offer specialized advice and assistance. They might also spend money on membership plans or online courses that provide access to specialized information and training. Billionaires make sure they have the resources and assistance they need to continue on their path of personal development by investing in these resources.

10.4.5 Acting and Putting Change into Practice

Putting money into one's own personal development goes beyond merely learning new things; it also involves making changes in one's life and acting upon them. Billionaires know that knowledge is not enough on its own; rather, growth and transformation come from applying knowledge. They actively look for chances to put what they've learned into practice and alter their attitudes, habits, and actions.

In order to successfully execute change, billionaires foster an environment that encourages personal development. They surround themselves with people who share their commitment to personal growth and who have similar values. To make sure they stay on track and hold themselves accountable to their personal growth goals, they could establish accountability partnerships or join mastermind groups.

10.4.6 Fostering a Growth Mentality

Billionaires develop a growth mentality as a foundational mindset to assist their own personal growth. They think that by working hard and being dedicated, they may improve their intelligence and abilities. They rise to challenges, see mistakes as teaching moments, and keep going in the face of difficulties.

They are aware that obstacles are transient and that they may always advance and develop.

Billionaires are able to embrace new opportunities and get over self-limiting beliefs by adopting a growth mentality. They welcome criticism and constructive criticism and see it as a chance for personal development. They view obstacles as chances for personal growth and tackle them with a positive outlook. Their ability to continuously learn, adjust, and develop thanks to this mentality guarantees their long-term success.

Throughout their lives, millionaires have made it a practice to emphasize investing in their own development. They are aware that personal development is an ongoing process of self-improvement rather than a final goal. Readers can also start on their own personal growth path and realize their full potential by creating goals, adopting a growth mindset, investing in personal development tools, taking action, and so on.

GIVING BACK
AND MAKING A
DIFFERENCE

11.1 The Significance of Charity

A significant part of the lives of billionaires and other affluent people is philanthropy. It emphasizes giving back to society and having a positive impact on the world rather than just accumulating wealth. This chapter will examine the value of generosity and its potential to foster individual development, societal advancement, and the establishment of enduring legacies.

11.1.1 Contributing to Society

The dedication of billionaires to contributing to society is one of their distinguishing traits. They are aware that the opportunities and support they have received from the community have contributed to their achievement in addition to their own efforts. Through philanthropy, they can show their appreciation and advance societal progress.

Billionaires can solve societal concerns, promote projects they are passionate about, and improve the lives of others by giving back. They decide to utilize their riches to make the world more just and equitable because they understand that it can be a powerful vehicle for change.

11.1.2 Making a Difference in Society

Writing checks and making donations is only one aspect of philanthropy; the other is producing a significant and long-lasting social impact. Billionaires know the value of investing in projects that have the potential to effect long-term change and contributing strategically.

To concentrate their philanthropic efforts, they frequently found foundations or other nonprofit institutions. These groups strive to achieve particular objectives, such as enhancing healthcare, education, or environmental sustainability. Billionaires make sure their resources are used wisely and leave a lasting impression on the communities they support by adopting a strategic approach.

11.1.3 Creating a Heritage

For billionaires, charity is about leaving a lasting legacy for future generations in addition to changing the world today. They are aware that wealth is determined by more than simply material possessions; it is also determined by the beneficial effects one has on society.

Billionaires have the ability to impact the world they leave behind through their philanthropic endeavors. In order to make sure that their legacy represents their interests and passions, they can support causes that are consistent with their values. This makes it possible for them to be recognized for the good changes they brought about in the world in addition to their financial success.

11.1.4 Changing the World for the Better

Billionaires have a rare opportunity to change the world in a meaningful way through philanthropy. It enables them to support creative solutions, deal with urgent social concerns, and give underprivileged people more influence.

Billionaires can address issues that governments and established institutions might find difficult to handle through their humanitarian endeavors. They are able to take chances, try out novel strategies, and effect change on a large enough scale to fundamentally alter society.

Billionaires feel a sense of fulfillment and purpose in changing the world, which transcends financial accomplishment. They are aware that genuine riches come from making a positive difference in other people's lives rather than merely accumulating cash.

In summary

A key component of the lives of billionaires and other affluent people is philanthropy. It enables people to change the world, leave a lasting legacy, contribute to society, and have a positive influence. Billionaires who are generous not only improve society but also find personal fulfillment and personal growth through their charitable endeavors. It's critical to acknowledge the value of generosity and its transformative potential as readers strive to follow in the billionaire's footsteps.

11.2 Making a Difference in Society

Making a difference in society is a key component of the billionaire mindset. While achieving financial success is frequently the main objective of billionaires, they also understand how important it is to use their power and resources to change the world for the better. In this section, we will look at the different ways that billionaires improve society and have an impact on society.

11.2.1 Giving Back to the Community through Philanthropy

Philanthropy is one of the most popular ways that billionaires make a difference in society. They are aware of the influence their wealth has and how it might be used to better the lives of others and address important societal issues. Billionaires frequently create foundations or philanthropic institutions to direct their wealth toward causes they fervently believe in.

Billionaires fund projects related to scientific research, healthcare, education, poverty alleviation, and the environment through philanthropy. They construct clinics and schools, provide for disaster relief operations, finance scholarships, and make investments in sustainable development initiatives. Billionaires want to enhance people's lives and bring about long-lasting change in their communities by giving back to them.

11.2.2 Social Entrepreneurship: Creating New Things to Benefit Society

Billionaires also use social entrepreneurship to improve society. They actively look for chances to solve social and environmental issues with creative solutions because they understand that business can be a potent force for good. Social entrepreneurs create sustainable models that address urgent concerns and yield financial returns by utilizing their resources and business expertise.

These business owners launch endeavors that put social and environmental goals ahead of financial success. They produce goods and services that empower underserved groups, solve unmet needs, and advance environmentally friendly behaviors. Billionaires help to create a more sustainable and just world by fusing their economic sense with a social commitment.

11.2.3 Policy Impact and Advocacy: Creating the Future

Billionaires also utilize their power to sway public opinion on significant social issues and push for legislative reforms. They are aware that their money and position give them a platform to raise their voices and effect significant systemic change. Billionaires participate in advocacy efforts to influence lawmakers and advance policies that are consistent with their vision for a better society by utilizing their networks and resources.

Billionaires endeavor to establish a conducive atmosphere for societal advancement by means of tactical collaborations with governmental bodies, non-governmental organizations, and additional interested parties. They participate in public awareness campaigns, fund research, assist think tanks, and organize support for subjects they are passionate about. Through their active involvement in the policy-making process, billionaires help to create a society that is more just and inclusive.

11.2.4 Impact Investing: Matching Assets to Principles

Impact investment is another way billionaires contribute to society. They understand that the social and environmental benefits of their investing choices sometimes outweigh the financial ones. Capital is allocated to companies and initiatives through impact investing with the goal of addressing social and environmental issues while generating profits.

Billionaires actively look for investment possibilities that support social advancement and are consistent with their principles. They put their money into businesses that place a high value on social responsibility, sustainability, and moral behavior. Billionaires are crucial in promoting innovation and expanding the reach of answers to worldwide problems through the allocation of their capital to worthwhile endeavors.

11.2.5 Ethical Business Practices and Corporate Social Responsibility

Billionaires are aware of the value of moral business conduct and corporate social responsibility (CSR). They understand that companies must conduct their operations in a way that maximizes positive effects on society and reduces negative ones. Billionaires make sure that social welfare, environmental sustainability, and moral behavior are given top priority by their businesses.

Billionaires lessen their environmental impact, foster employee well-being, and assist local communities through CSR activities. They promote diversity and inclusion, uphold fair labor standards, and aid in the advancement of the local community. Billionaires show their dedication to making a good impact through their businesses by incorporating social and environmental concerns into their business plans.

To sum up, billionaires actively work to improve society and recognize the importance of having a positive social influence.

Billionaires utilize charity, social entrepreneurship, impact investing, advocacy, and moral business conduct to solve urgent social challenges and promote constructive change. Readers may make an effect and help create a more sustainable and fair world by taking up a similar mindset and implementing social impact into their own lives.

11.3 Creating a Heritage

The idea of leaving a legacy transcends tangible wealth and success in business. Making a difference in other people's lives and having a long-lasting effect on the globe are the goals. Billionaires are aware of the value of leaving a lasting legacy and work hard to make a difference that lasts far longer than their own lives.

11.3.1 Establishing Your Heritage

Establishing your personal definition of a legacy is crucial before you can begin creating one. Legacy is a very personal idea that means different things to different people. While some may describe their legacy as building a prosperous commercial empire, others would place more emphasis on charitable contributions and contributing to society. Think carefully about your beliefs, interests, and the legacy you wish to leave behind.

11.3.2 Matching Your Behavior to Your Principles

Making sure that your activities are consistent with your beliefs is essential if you want to leave a legacy that is in line with your ideals. To understand your basic principles and how they might direct your decisions and actions, you must engage in introspection and self-reflection. You will find fulfillment and a sense of purpose in your work when your actions are in line with your values, and this will add to the legacy you are creating.

11.3.3 Changing the World in Your Community

A significant way to leave a lasting impression is by contributing to your neighborhood. Billionaires actively look for ways to improve society because they recognize how important it is to give back to the community. This can be accomplished by volunteering, giving to charitable causes, or supporting causes near and dear to your heart. You have the power to make a long-lasting difference in the lives of others by devoting your time, money, and experience to projects that promote good change.

11.3.4 Giving Others Mentoring and Empowerment

Mentoring and empowering others is an additional means of leaving a lasting legacy. Billionaires understand the need to pass on their wisdom and experiences to the next generation of leaders. You can encourage and direct people on their own journeys to achievement by taking on the role of mentor. Encouraging people to realize their greatest potential helps them as well as the legacy you are creating. Your own legacy is enhanced when you support and encourage the success of others.

11.3.5 Coming Up with Long-Term Fixes

Developing long-lasting answers to the problems and difficulties society faces is part of leaving a legacy. Billionaires are aware of the value of long-term planning and creative problem-solving. You can bring about long-lasting change that will help present and future generations by concentrating on sustainable solutions. Developing sustainable solutions, whether via digital breakthroughs, social entrepreneurship, or environmental initiatives, is essential to leaving a lasting legacy.

11.3.6 Motivating and Inspiring Others

Leaving a lasting legacy involves more than simply your own accomplishments; it also involves encouraging and motivating others to realize their own potential. Billionaires use their understanding of influence to motivate and encourage people around them. By telling others about your experiences—both triumphs and setbacks—you inspire them to overcome obstacles and pursue greatness. By motivating people to reach their objectives, you leave a legacy of success and empowerment.

11.3.7 Making a Permanent Impression

In the end, creating a legacy is about changing the world in a way that will last. Billionaires try to make the most of their limited time on earth by leaving a lasting and positive legacy. They recognize this. This can be accomplished in a number of ways, including by developing cutting-edge goods and services, promoting social change, and funding research and education. You can make sure that your legacy will continue to change the world long after you are gone by making a lasting impression.

11.3.8 Ongoing Development and Adjustment

Leaving a legacy takes ongoing development and adaptation; it is not a one-time feat. Billionaires know that in order to leave a lasting legacy, they must change with the times and adapt to the ever-changing environment. This means continuing to be inquisitive, accepting of novel concepts, and receptive to growth and learning. You can make sure that your legacy is still relevant and has an impact by always pushing the envelope and challenging yourself.

11.3.9 Honoring Your Heritage

It is crucial to take the time to recognize your accomplishments and the difference you have made as you forge your legacy. Recognize the achievements you have made and the lives you have impacted. Honoring your legacy acts as a reminder of the good change you have brought about, in addition to giving you a sense of fulfillment. It may also encourage others to carry on the job you have begun by following in your footsteps.

Leaving a legacy takes a lifetime of hard work, passion, and determination to change the world. You may leave a lasting legacy that goes much beyond your own life by establishing your legacy, acting in a way that is consistent with your beliefs, and making a conscious effort to make a positive difference. Recall that leaving a lasting legacy involves more than simply your accomplishments; it also involves the lives you touch and the good things you bring about in the world.

11.4 Changing the World for the Better

Although this book's earlier chapters have emphasized accumulating wealth and achieving personal achievement, it's crucial to keep in mind that genuine fulfillment originates from changing the world. This chapter examines how billionaires utilize their influence to make a lasting difference. Billionaires have the ability and means to affect positive change on a global scale.

11.4.1 The Influence of Contribution

A prominent attribute of billionaires is their unwavering dedication to philanthropy. They are aware that prosperity entails using one's resources to better the lives of others in addition to personal benefit. Giving back is a means of leaving a good legacy in addition to being morally right. Billionaires frequently create foundations or philanthropic groups to promote issues that are close to their hearts, including environmental preservation, healthcare, education, and poverty reduction. Their goal in making these investments is to address systemic problems and bring about long-lasting change.

11.4.2 Using Power to Achieve Social Impact

Billionaires possess a special capacity to sway public opinion and direct legislative action. They realize that they have an obligation to promote social change as a result of their riches and status. Numerous billionaires make use of their platforms to bring attention to significant problems and organize funding to solve them. They work together to promote social impact and build a more just society with governments, non-governmental organizations, and other stakeholders. Billionaires can raise the voices of underrepresented groups and support issues that might not otherwise receive attention by using their power.

11.4.3 Coming Up with Long-Term Solutions

Billionaires understand that solving complicated societal issues with money alone is insufficient. They recognize how critical it is to develop long-lasting solutions that deal with the underlying causes of these problems. This calls for a long-term strategic approach rather than band-aid solutions. Billionaires can help develop new technologies, business models, and social businesses that have the potential to bring about long-lasting change by funding research and innovation. They also work together with authorities and influential people to find novel ideas and promote systemic change.

11.4.4 Giving Others Power

Billionaires know that the real influence comes from giving others the tools they need to effect change. They understand that young leaders, business owners, and social activists may benefit from their money and experience. Billionaires have the power to change people's lives and help them reach their full potential by lending their networks, resources, and expertise. They offer financial support for training and educational initiatives, chances for mentorship, and entry into networks that might lead to possibilities for those who want to make a difference. Billionaires have an impact that goes well beyond their own deeds when they empower others.

11.4.5 Care of the Environment

Billionaires not only deal with social issues but also understand the value of environmental care. They are aware of the close connection between human welfare and the state of the world. To lessen the effects of climate change and save natural resources, many billionaires make investments in sustainable agriculture, renewable energy, and conservation initiatives. Billionaires contribute to a future that is more robust and sustainable for future generations by sponsoring programs that promote environmental sustainability.

11.4.6 Motivating Others to Contribute

Billionaires have the ability to encourage and inspire people to contribute back. Through their deeds and charitable pursuits, they serve as role models for people from many backgrounds. Billionaires have the power to motivate people to take action and improve their local communities by sharing their personal stories and emphasizing the positive effects of their donations. They question traditional conventions surrounding wealth acquisition and utilize their influence to promote a giving culture. Billionaires have the power to inspire a new generation of changemakers by advocating for a more compassionate and inclusive view of wealth.

To sum up, a key component of the millionaire mindset is wanting to change the world. Billionaires know that their real success is determined by their beneficial social influence in addition to their financial wealth. Billionaires have the ability to create a lasting legacy that extends beyond their own lives through giving back, using their influence, developing sustainable solutions, empowering others, and encouraging environmental stewardship. Regardless of your financial situation, you, as readers of this book, have the ability to change the world in your own unique way. Accept the wisdom of the world's billionaires and apply it to improve both your own and other people's lives.

CONCLUSION

12.1 Taking Stock of Your Individual Path

It is crucial that you pause at the end of this book to consider your own personal path. You have been exposed to the routines and thinking of billionaires throughout the chapters, and you have gained knowledge on how to incorporate these ideas into your own life. It's time to take a moment to evaluate your progress and the changes you've made.

12.1.1 Honoring Your Accomplishments

Celebrate your accomplishments for a time. Recognize the actions you have taken to advance your achievement and personal development. Acknowledge the positive improvements you have made in your life and the habits you have created. Honoring your accomplishments is about recognizing your own development and advancement rather than bragging or looking for approval from others. You can increase your self-assurance and drive to carry on with your journey in this way.

12.1.2 Evaluating Your Difficulties

Consider the difficulties you have encountered thus far. Think back to the challenges that have put your tenacity and resolve to the test. Evaluate your response to these problems and the lessons you took away from them. Recall that failures and setbacks are chances for improvement rather than indicators of defeat. Accept the knowledge you've gained from your setbacks and utilize it to your advantage going forward.

12.1.3 Finding Opportunities for Development

Without identifying areas that require work, no journey towards personal change is complete. Examine your habits and yourself honestly. Are there any areas left for you to develop further? Do you have any habits that you should improve or break? Finding places for improvement shows a dedication to ongoing development and self-improvement rather than weakness. Seize the chance to further hone your routines and perspective.

12.1.4 Reviewing Your Objectives

Go back to the objectives you set for yourself at the start of this adventure. Have you succeeded in achieving them? Have your objectives altered or evolved over time? Take some time to review your objectives and make any required changes. Recall that objectives are dynamic and should be modified in response to personal development. Take this time to ponder and reevaluate your objectives in light of your values and aspirations at the moment.

12.1.5 Expressing Thanks and Recognition

Give thanks and show appreciation for the experience you have had. Consider for a moment the individuals who have helped you along the way, the resources you have at your disposal, and the opportunities that have presented themselves. Practicing gratitude is a powerful way to change your perspective and attract more positive energy into your life. You may develop an attitude of abundance and draw in additional chances for development and achievement by expressing your thanks.

12.1.6 Formulating a Course of Action

It's time to make an action plan for the future now that you have given some thought to your own journey. Determine the habits and mental changes you wish to keep fostering based on your reflections. Establish measurable objectives that are consistent with your vision for success. Divide these objectives into more doable, smaller tasks that you may complete each day or each week. You may make sure that your journey toward personal improvement continues after reading this book by putting together an action plan.

12.1.7 Taking Up Lifelong Education

Recall that personal development is an ongoing process. Adopt a lifetime learning mindset and make a commitment to keep learning new things and developing your abilities. Look for new ways to learn, whether through mentors, books, classes, or other experiences. Accept the unfamiliar and keep an open mind to fresh viewpoints. You can make sure that your personal journey is dynamic and full of growth and discovery by embracing lifelong learning.

12.1.8 Remaining Devoted to Your Path

Lastly, resolve to continue on this path of self-improvement. Recognize that things won't always be simple and that you can experience doubts or failures. But keep in mind the behaviors and perspectives of billionaires that you have read about in this book. Remain dedicated to your objectives and the routines that will help you succeed. As you travel, surround yourself with a network of like-minded people who will encourage and support you.

As you wrap up this book, keep in mind that you are still on the path to personal growth. It is an ongoing process of development and self-improvement rather than a goal. Accept the routines and outlook of billionaires, and allow them to lead you to an incredible life of fulfillment and achievement. You have the ability to design the life you want, and you may achieve your objectives and lead an abundant life by thinking back on your own experience, acting, and remaining dedicated.

12.2 Acting and Putting Change into Practice

Taking initiative and putting change into practice are critical milestones on the path to success. This book's concluding portion will include useful tactics and doable actions that will give you the confidence to transform your life for the better. You may change your life and succeed beyond belief by taking on the routines and mindset of billionaires.

12.2.1 Clearly Determining Objectives

Establishing precise, measurable goals is one of the first stages of putting change into practice. It is easy to become disoriented or lose motivation when traveling without a clear plan. Spend some time defining and documenting your long- and short-term objectives. Writing down your goals enhances your dedication to them and gives them a more concrete form.

Once your objectives are established, divide them into more manageable, smaller tasks. They will become less daunting and simpler to handle as a result. To hold yourself responsible and monitor your development, make an action plan or schedule. To stay on course and make sure your goals are in line with your overarching vision, evaluate and tweak them frequently.

12.2.2 Acting with Consistency

Taking persistent action is essential to bringing about change and accomplishing your objectives. It is insufficient to only have goals; you also need to act on them with intention and consistency. Create a daily schedule with specified tasks that are in line with your objectives. This could include setting aside a specified period of time each day to work on a habit or task that will help you achieve your objectives.

Don't put things off, and maintain your discipline. While it is easy to become sidetracked or disheartened along the path, successful people know how crucial it is to maintain commitment and focus. Seek strategies for maintaining your motivation, such as affirmations, visualization, or surrounding yourself with supportive people who share your values.

12.2.3 Accepting Adaptability and Change

Accepting change is a prerequisite for putting it into practice. Be receptive to fresh insights, viewpoints, and chances. Successful people are aware that change is a given and that it's essential to adjust to changing conditions in order to advance. Be prepared to explore new things and venture outside of your comfort zone. Accept failure as a teaching tool and apply it to improve your strategy.

Adopt a growth mentality that interprets obstacles as chances for personal development. Consider setbacks as stepping stones towards progress rather than as failures. Develop tenacity and resilience by understanding that obstacles are transient and can be surmounted with willpower and an optimistic outlook.

12.2.4 Looking for Assistance and Responsibility

It might be difficult to implement change, but your chances of success can be significantly increased if you have a support structure in place. Look for coaches, mentors, or like-minded people who can offer accountability, direction, and support. Those who encourage and inspire you to realize your full potential should be in your immediate vicinity.

Taking responsibility for changes is essential. Join a mastermind group or find an accountability partner so you can check in and discuss your progress on a regular basis. This outside accountability can offer insightful criticism and encouragement while keeping you on course.

12.2.5 Honoring Significant Events and Examining Advancements

It's critical to recognize and celebrate your accomplishments as you move forward and execute change. Recognizing little victories along the way increases drive and strengthens constructive behaviors. Give yourself some time to consider your progress and the lessons you have discovered. By reflecting on your progress, you may recognize your changes and modify your strategy as needed.

Review your objectives and your progress on a regular basis. Are you moving in the right direction? Do you need to modify or make any additions? Take advantage of this time for introspection to improve your tactics and maintain alignment with your goals.

12.2.6 Ongoing Education and Development

Change implementation is a continuous process rather than a one-time occurrence. People who are successful recognize the value of lifelong learning and development. Make a commitment to lifelong learning and look for chances to increase your knowledge and abilities. Take classes, go to seminars, read books, and look for mentors who can guide you in your development.

Always be inquisitive and receptive, looking for fresh approaches to development and innovation. Accept constructive criticism and comments as chances for personal development. Push your boundaries and venture outside of your comfort zone on a regular basis.

12.2.7 Acting Currently

It's time to act now that you have a better understanding of the routines and thinking of billionaires. Change implementation calls for dedication, self-control, and a readiness to push oneself beyond comfort zones. Establish specific objectives, act consistently, welcome change, look for help, acknowledge accomplishments, and never stop learning and growing.

Recall that success does not come easily. It's a path that takes commitment and tenacity. Remain committed to your goal and never lose sight of your extraordinary potential. You have the ability to change your life and succeed beyond measure by emulating the habits of millionaires and putting the techniques in this book into practice. Take the first step toward your own success by acting now.

12.3 Proceeding on the Road to Achievement
Best wishes! This is the last chapter of the book, "Continuing the Path to Success." You are now aware of the significance of personal growth, the influence of habits, the thinking of billionaires, and the path to success. A wide range of topics have also been covered, including time management, resilience, creative thinking, forging strong bonds with others, cultivating a growth mentality, taking prudent risks, establishing a wealth mindset, adhering to a routine of discipline and consistency, accepting lifelong learning, and giving back.

In this last section, we'll talk about how you can keep moving forward on your success path and keep the mindset and habits you've built throughout this book. Recall that success is a lifelong journey rather than a destination. It calls for ongoing development, adaptability, and effort. Now let's get started and investigate how you may keep moving forward on your path to success.

12.3.1 Welcome to Lifelong Education

A fundamental practice of billionaires is their dedication to lifelong learning. They are aware that information is power and that continuing to be curious and receptive is crucial for both career and personal development. As you proceed on your successful journey, resolve to embrace lifelong learning. Seek out fresh information, investigate other viewpoints, and keep abreast of the most recent trends and advancements in the industry.

Take online classes, read books, go to seminars and workshops, and have in-depth discussions with mentors and experts. Recall that schooling is not the only way to learn. It can occur in a variety of settings and ways. Continue to be a voracious learner and never give up on chances to broaden your knowledge and expertise.

12.3.2 Make New Objectives and Challenges

Achieving success is a dynamic process rather than a static condition. Setting new objectives when you reach your current ones will help you stay motivated and involved. Take some time to consider your past experiences and come up with fresh objectives and difficulties that are consistent with your vision and core beliefs.

Establish SMART (specific, measurable, achievable, relevant, and time-bound) goals for both the short and long term. Divide your objectives into more manageable benchmarks and devise practical strategies to reach them. Never forget to push yourself and venture outside of your comfort zone. When you take on new difficulties and push yourself beyond your comfort zone, you grow.

12.3.3 Embrace the Positive Influences Around You

The individuals you choose to spend time with and surround yourself with greatly influence your success, habits, and way of thinking. As you proceed down your successful road, surround yourself with people who inspire and motivate you. Look for people that match your values and goals to serve as mentors, role models, and like-minded folks.

Take part in thought-provoking discussions, work together on projects, and pick up tips from others who have previously accomplished what you want. Being in the company of positive people will not only offer you insightful advice and helpful insights, but it will also help you build a network of support that will enable you to overcome setbacks and recognize your accomplishments.

12.3.4 Engage in Self-Reflection and Assessment

Frequent introspection and assessment are essential for developing oneself. Spend some time thinking back on your development, successes, and areas that still need work. Honor your accomplishments and take note of the lessons you've learned from your mistakes and disappointments.

Consider asking yourself important questions like, "What have I accomplished so far?" What are my advantages and disadvantages? What adjustments can I make to get better results? How can I match my behavior to my objectives and values? You can remain on course and carry on developing and changing if you periodically assess your progress and make the required corrections.

12.3.5 Remain Dedicated and Unwavering

Achieving success takes time. It calls for dedication, tenacity, and fortitude. On your journey to achievement, you will encounter obstacles, disappointments, and periods of uncertainty. But it's crucial to stick with your objectives and keep going when things get tough.

Recall that failure is a chance to grow and learn, not the end. Accept failure as a necessary step on the path to success, and turn it into an opportunity to get better. Even when things are difficult, don't waver from your goals, outlook, and forward motion. You will eventually achieve the achievement you want thanks to your dedication and perseverance.

12.3.6 Honor Your Successes

It's critical to recognize and appreciate your accomplishments as you proceed down your path to success. Spend some time appreciating and acknowledging your accomplishments, no matter how tiny. Honoring your accomplishments strengthens your good behaviors and outlook while also increasing your motivation and self-assurance.

Give yourself a reward when you accomplish goals, finish projects, and overcome obstacles. Celebrate with your loved ones, close friends, or support system. By acknowledging and appreciating your accomplishments, you establish a positive feedback loop that increases your drive and advances you on the path to success.

12.3.7 Reinvest and change the world.

Finally, keep in mind the value of contributing to society and changing the world as you proceed down your successful path. Make a positive social impact and contribute to charities that share your values by using your success and influence.

Seek opportunities to give back and impart your skills, resources, and experiences, whether through volunteering, philanthropy, or mentoring others. Not only does it provide you with a sense of purpose and fulfillment, but it also leaves a legacy that goes beyond your personal achievements.

12.4 Concluding Remarks and Motivation

Congratulations for finishing "The 10 Habits of Billionaires: Powerful Lessons in Personal Change," which has been a life-changing experience. You now possess insightful knowledge, useful tactics, and a mindset that will help you achieve remarkable accomplishments.

Recall that success is a lifelong journey rather than a destination. It necessitates lifelong learning, goal-setting, being surrounded by positive influences, self-reflection practice, commitment and persistence, celebrating victories, and giving back.

As you proceed towards achievement, adopt the routines and perspectives of multibillionaires. Be inventive, resilient, and self-disciplined. Develop solid bonds with others, rise to difficulties, take measured chances, and make an investment in your own development. Above all, have faith in your own abilities to design the life you want.

It's now time for you to put what you've learned in this book into practice. Be consistent, start small, and keep in mind that every step matters. The road to success is now yours to travel. I wish you luck!

12.4 Concluding Remarks and Motivation

Best wishes! This concludes "The 10 Habits of Billionaires: Powerful Lessons in Personal Change." We have studied the thinking and habits of the most successful people in the world throughout this book. We have examined the routines that billionaires have developed to lead very successful lives. It's time to take stock of your individual journey and use it as motivation to make the adjustments required for your own achievement.

12.4.1 Accepting Your Individual Journey

You have learned a great deal about the routines and thinking of billionaires as you have read through the chapters in this book. It's crucial to keep in mind, though, that success varies from person to person. Every person must choose their own special course to take. While it's helpful to draw lessons from other people's experiences, it's just as crucial to accept your own path and measure success according to your own standards.

12.4.2 The Strength of Willpower

The unshakable determination of millionaires is one thing they have in common. They are aware that failures and setbacks are inevitable on any road and that success rarely comes easily. They can keep going forward and conquer challenges because of their perseverance. As you set out on your own route to success, keep in mind that perseverance is essential. Accept obstacles as teaching opportunities, have a positive outlook, and persevere in the face of difficulty. Any challenge you face can be overcome if you are persistent enough.

12.4.3 Fostering an Attitude of Growth

We have stressed the significance of cultivating a growth mindset throughout this book. Billionaires know that brains and skills can be acquired with commitment and hard work. They welcome challenges, look for chances to learn, and persevere in the face of difficulties. You can realize your greatest potential and experience remarkable success by embracing a growth mindset. Never back down from a task that has the potential to propel you to new heights. Have faith in your capacity to learn and grow.

12.4.4 Acting and Putting Change into Practice

Acquiring knowledge by itself is insufficient for success. What will actually alter your life are the steps you take and the adjustments you make. It is important that you act upon the lessons you have learned from this book and put the routines and techniques that speak to you into practice. Take steady steps toward your success vision by starting small and establishing clear goals. Recall that daily behaviors and activities are what add up to big results over time.

12.4.5 Ongoing Education and Development

The path to success is a lifelong process rather than a final destination. Billionaires recognize the value of lifelong learning and development. They read a lot, seek out information, and surround themselves with role models and mentors. As you put this book down, make a commitment to lifelong study and development. Take advantage of new possibilities, increase your knowledge, and never give up on your goal of getting better. Your chances of attaining amazing achievements increase with the amount of money you put into your personal development.

12.4.6 Changing the World for the Better

Finally, keep in mind the significance of changing the world as you set out on your own path to success. Billionaires are aware that making a positive difference in the lives of people and society at large brings greater joy than simply accumulating wealth. Seek opportunities to give back, support causes that are important to you, and utilize your success to inspire others. You can leave a lasting legacy that goes much beyond material prosperity by changing the world.

12.4.7 Your Adventure Is About to Begin

It's time to apply everything you've learned to your own life now that you've finished reading this book. Recall that success is a journey rather than a destination. Accept your individual route, keep going when things get tough, and develop a growth mentality. Act, put changes into place, and make a commitment to lifelong learning and development. Above all, make an effort to change the world. The road to success is now yours to travel. Take it on with fervor, tenacity, and a resolute faith in your own abilities. You possess the ability to attain remarkable accomplishments and establish a prosperous and satisfying life.